GUN VIOLENCE

OPPOSING VIEWPOINTS®

Other Books of Related Interest

GUN VIOLENCE

OPPOSING VIEWPOINTS®

Margaret Haerens, *Book Editor*

Bonnie Szumski, *Publisher*
Helen Cothran, *Managing Editor*

OPPOSING
VIEWPOINTS®
SERIES

GREENHAVEN PRESS
An imprint of Thomson Gale, a part of The Thomson Corporation

THOMSON
GALE

Detroit • New York • San Francisco • San Diego • New Haven, Conn.
Waterville, Maine • London • Munich

For more information, contact
Greenhaven Press
27500 Drake Rd.
Farmington Hills, MI 48331-3535
Or you can visit our Internet site at http://www.gale.com

Greenhaven Press anthologies primarily consist of previously published material taken from a variety of sources, including periodicals, books, scholarly journals, newspapers, government documents, and position papers from private and public organizations. These original sources are often edited for length and to ensure their accessibility for a young adult audience. The anthology editors also change the original titles of these works in order to clearly present the main thesis of each viewpoint and to explicitly indicate the opinion presented in the viewpoint. These alterations are made in consideration of both the reading and comprehension levels of a young adult audience. Every effort is made to ensure that Greenhaven Press accurately reflects the original intent of the authors included in this anthology.

LIBRARY OF CONGRESS CATALOGING-IN-PUBLICATION DATA	
Gun violence / Margaret Haerens, book editor.	
p. cm. — (Opposing viewpoints series)	
Includes bibliographical references and index.	
ISBN 0-7377-3354-3 (lib. : alk. paper) — ISBN 0-7377-3355-1 (pbk. : alk. paper)	
1. Gun control—United States. 2. Violent crimes—United States. 3. Firearms ownership—Government policy—United States. I. Haerens, Margaret. II. Opposing viewpoints series (Unnumbered)	
HV7436.G8756 2006	
363.330973—dc22	2005052807

"Congress shall make
no law...abridging the
freedom of speech, or of
the press."

First Amendment to the U.S. Constitution

The basic foundation of our democracy is the First
Amendment guarantee of freedom of expression.
The Opposing Viewpoints Series is dedicated to the
concept of this basic freedom and the idea that it is
more important to practice it than to enshrine it.

Contents

Chapter 3: Does the Constitution Protect Private Gun Ownership?

Chapter 4: How Can Gun Violence Be Reduced?

Why Consider Opposing Viewpoints?

"The only way in which a human being can make some approach to knowing the whole of a subject is by hearing what can be said about it by persons of every variety of opinion and studying all modes in which it can be looked at by every character of mind. No wise man ever acquired his wisdom in any mode but this."

John Stuart Mill

In our media-intensive culture it is not difficult to find differing opinions. Thousands of newspapers and magazines and dozens of radio and television talk shows resound with differing points of view. The difficulty lies in deciding which opinion to agree with and which "experts" seem the most credible. The more inundated we become with differing opinions and claims, the more essential it is to hone critical reading and thinking skills to evaluate these ideas. Opposing Viewpoints books address this problem directly by presenting stimulating debates that can be used to enhance and teach these skills. The varied opinions contained in each book examine many different aspects of a single issue. While examining these conveniently edited opposing views, readers can develop critical thinking skills such as the ability to compare and contrast authors' credibility, facts, argumentation styles, use of persuasive techniques, and other stylistic tools. In short, the Opposing Viewpoints Series is an ideal way to attain the higher-level thinking and reading skills so essential in a culture of diverse and contradictory opinions.

In addition to providing a tool for critical thinking, Opposing Viewpoints books challenge readers to question their own strongly held opinions and assumptions. Most people form their opinions on the basis of upbringing, peer pressure, and personal, cultural, or professional bias. By reading carefully balanced opposing views, readers must directly confront new ideas as well as the opinions of those with whom they disagree. This is not to simplistically argue that everyone who reads opposing views will—or should—change his or her opinion. Instead, the series enhances readers' understanding of their own views by encouraging confrontation with opposing ideas. Careful examination of others' views can lead to the readers' understanding of the logical inconsistencies in their own opinions, perspective on why they hold an opinion, and the consideration of the possibility that their opinion requires further evaluation.

Evaluating Other Opinions

To ensure that this type of examination occurs, Opposing Viewpoints books present all types of opinions. Prominent spokespeople on different sides of each issue as well as well-known professionals from many disciplines challenge the reader. An additional goal of the series is to provide a forum for other, less known, or even unpopular viewpoints. The opinion of an ordinary person who has had to make the decision to cut off life support from a terminally ill relative, for example, may be just as valuable and provide just as much insight as a medical ethicist's professional opinion. The editors have two additional purposes in including these less known views. One, the editors encourage readers to respect others' opinions—even when not enhanced by professional credibility. It is only by reading or listening to and objectively evaluating others' ideas that one can determine whether they are worthy of consideration. Two, the inclusion of such viewpoints encourages the important critical thinking skill of objectively evaluating an author's credentials and bias. This evaluation will illuminate an author's reasons for taking a particular stance on an issue and will aid in readers' evaluation of the author's ideas.

It is our hope that these books will give readers a deeper understanding of the issues debated and an appreciation of the complexity of even seemingly simple issues when good and honest people disagree. This awareness is particularly important in a democratic society such as ours in which people enter into public debate to determine the common good. Those with whom one disagrees should not be regarded as enemies but rather as people whose views deserve careful examination and may shed light on one's own.

Thomas Jefferson once said that "difference of opinion leads to inquiry, and inquiry to truth." Jefferson, a broadly educated man, argued that "if a nation expects to be ignorant and free . . . it expects what never was and never will be." As individuals and as a nation, it is imperative that we consider the opinions of others and examine them with skill and discernment. The Opposing Viewpoints Series is intended to help readers achieve this goal.

David L. Bender and Bruno Leone,
Founders

Introduction

"At its heart, the gun debate is a question about the relationship between the citizen, the state's power to regulate, and the maintenance of public order."
—*Robert J. Spitzer, author of*
The Politics of Gun Control

Gun control has been a controversial issue in the United States since the first attempt to pass gun control legislation in the 1930s. It was then that an effort to reduce crime resulted in an unsuccessful attempt by President Franklin D. Roosevelt to pass legislation that would require the registration of handguns. The assassination of President John F. Kennedy in 1963 once again catapulted the gun control debate to the forefront of American consciousness. The public outcry after Kennedy's death led to the Gun Control Act of 1968, which expanded gun-dealer licensing requirements and banned some felons, illegal drug users, and mentally challenged persons from purchasing firearms. After the attempted assassination of President Ronald Reagan in 1981, gun control activists once again called for tighter restrictions on gun sales, arguing that the Gun Control Act of 1968 was not stringent enough. They lobbied for a waiting period, during which background checks could be performed on all gun purchasers in the United States. Named after James Brady, Reagan's press secretary, who was severely injured during the assassination attempt, the Brady Bill became law in 1993.

As these events illustrate, the gun control debate has been shaped by high-profile events and the ideologies of sitting presidents. When crime rates rise or highly publicized shootings occur, calls for increased gun control become more vociferous. When those who support gun rights are elected president or form a majority in Congress, gun rights legislation is rarely passed. When those in power favor gun control, new bills to regulate firearms often become law. In recent years three events have had an especially strong impact on the gun control debate.

The first event was the April 1999 shooting at Columbine

High School in Littleton, Colorado, which is known as the deadliest school shooting in American history. Illegally obtaining a semiautomatic handgun and two sawed-off shotguns, two teens killed twelve students and one teacher, injured twenty-four others, and then committed suicide. This tragedy reinvigorated the debate over the availability of guns. Horrified by the senseless killing in Colorado, hundreds of thousands of gun control activists and supporters gathered in Washington, D.C., in May 2000 to participate in the Million Mom March. The march was a call for stricter gun control legislation, especially laws that would keep firearms out of the hands of children.

The second event to impact the gun control debate was the election of President George W. Bush in 2000. His opponent, Al Gore, was vocal about his support for gun control legislation, and he made gun control a central component of his presidential campaign. Bush, a gun rights supporter, garnered the support of influential lobbying groups such as the National Rifle Association. He became the recipient of not only the NRA's financial support, but also the support of a range of pro-gun groups and the powerful gun industry. Many commentators claim that this support helped Bush win the election. With a gun rights supporter in the White House, and Republicans, who usually oppose gun laws, in control of the Senate and House of Representatives, it was assured that no significant gun control legislation would be proposed or passed over the next few years.

The third major event was the terrorist attacks on the World Trade Center and the Pentagon on September 11, 2001. In the aftermath of the attacks, handgun sales skyrocketed. The Federal Bureau of Investigation reported that it performed 455,000 additional background checks for handgun purchases in the six months following the September 11 attacks than it had during the same period in 2000. The attacks also resulted in a national debate on the ease with which terrorists might obtain firearms in America. Lax background checking procedures at gun shows led to legislation to close the "gun-show loophole." The law would require that all purchasers, even individuals at gun shows, be subject to a background check before they could purchase a firearm.

Backers of the legislation argued that it would prevent known criminals and terrorists from obtaining guns. However, gun rights advocates argued that supporters of such legislation were exploiting the September 11 attacks in order to pass draconian new gun control laws that would encroach on the rights of law-abiding Americans. They argued that in such uncertain times, it was more important than ever to respect the right of Americans to protect themselves and their country. The Senate and the House of Representatives are still reviewing the Gun Show Loophole Closing Act of 2003.

As these three examples illustrate, shootings, national elections, and terrorist attacks have profound impacts on the gun control debate. The authors of the viewpoints presented in *Opposing Viewpoints: Gun Violence* discuss many of these events in the following chapters: How Serious Is the Problem of Gun Violence? Does Private Gun Ownership Reduce the Threat of Gun Violence? Does the Constitution Protect Private Gun Ownership? How Can Gun Violence Be Reduced? The information provided in this volume will provide insight into how political and social events shape the gun control debate and help determine what laws are passed to address gun violence.

CHAPTER 1

How Serious Is the Problem of Gun Violence?

Chapter Preface

Each year, more than twenty-eight thousand Americans die in gun suicides, homicides, and unintentional shootings. In recent years there has been a growing segment of experts and activists who view the problem of firearm violence as a public heath issue. In 1983 the Centers for Disease Control and Prevention (CDC) first declared guns a threat to public health and created a violence epidemiology branch to study the problem. Despite the fact that the CDC has taken a strong position on this issue, it is far from settled. While many experts support the CDC's stance, countless others disagree.

David Hemenway, director of Harvard's Injury Control Research Center and Youth Violence Prevention Center, calls the prevalence of gun violence in the United States a modern-day public health epidemic. In order to address this epidemic, advocates of the public health approach strive to make people understand that guns are a consumer product, like cars, aspirin bottles, and cigarette lighters. Many experts believe that guns could be made safer, and argue that government regulation can play a crucial role in this effort. Hemenway asserts that "it has become increasingly recognized that the most promising approach to reduce firearm injury is to emphasize prevention, focus on the community, use a broad array of policies, and bring together diverse interest groups." This proactive and collective approach to gun violence is considered by some experts to be the best hope for significantly reducing gun violence. The first step, they assert, is changing the belief that lethal violence is a normal and acceptable part of everyday American life.

Opponents of this view contend that public health advocates have one goal: to enact stringent new gun control measures aimed to limit individuals' access to firearms. These critics point out that the most vocal supporters of the public health approach to gun violence are those who have long advocated for stricter gun control laws. Denying that gun violence is epidemic, critics say gun control advocates have exaggerated the issue in order to sway public opinion and help get draconian gun control legislation passed. Miguel A. Faria Jr., editor in chief of the *Medical Sentinel*, argues that "when it [comes] to the portrayal of firearms and violence, and the gun control 'research' promulgated by public-health officials, it [is] obvious that the medical literature [is] biased, riddled with serious errors in facts, logic, and methodology, and thus utterly unreliable." Critics of the public health approach maintain that focusing on guns does nothing but distract people from issues such as inner-city poverty and unemployment, which they view as the prime causes of violence of all kinds.

Although support for the public health approach to gun violence has grown, many experts still criticize the approach. The authors in the following viewpoint debate other issues concerning the prevalence of gun violence. As the controversy over the public health approach to firearms violence shows, determining the seriousness of gun violence is contentious.

"The public policy and public health consequences of gun injuries are substantial."

Gun Violence Is a Serious Problem

Robert Spitzer

In the following viewpoint, excerpted from his book *The Politics of Gun Control*, Robert Spitzer argues that the United States experiences more gun violence than any other developed nation. Guns account for tens of thousands of deaths each year, he contends. Moreover, firearms are responsible for even more injuries, he maintains. Spitzer is a distinguished service professor of political science at the State University of New York, College at Cortland. He is a frequent commentator on political and gun-related issues, and has written or edited ten books on American politics and the right to bear arms.

As you read, consider the following questions:
1. Why do some people want to view gun violence as a public health issue, in Spitzer's opinion?
2. According to Spitzer, what percentage of homicides and suicides are committed with guns?
3. What demographics are hit hardest by gun violence in America, in the author's view?

Case 1: On 14 October 1989, three teenage boys were examining a .38-caliber automatic pistol that belonged to the father of one of the boys. Thinking that the gun was unloaded because the ammunition magazine had been removed, one of the boys pulled the trigger, accidentally shooting and killing fourteen-year-old Michael J. Steber of Clay, New York. The boys had not realized that a round was still in the gun's chamber. Two years later, the parents of the dead boy filed a civil suit against the gun's owner (and father of the shooter), Gordon Lane, a former Syracuse police officer and head of the state's chapter of Vietnam Veterans of America, and against the gun manufacturer for failing to include a 75-cent safety feature that would have prevented the gun from firing without the ammunition clip. Lane had several guns in the home and had guided his son's use of them. The father of the dead boy questioned the justification for keeping such weapons in the home. "I'm a Vietnam veteran too," said Mr. Steber, "and I don't have a gun around the house. I don't need it."

Case 2: One evening, Marion Hammer was on her way to her car located in a parking garage in Tallahassee, Florida, when she noticed a car carrying six drunken men following her. Less than five feet tall and weighing 111 pounds, she feared trouble when some of the men made comments that amounted to a threat of rape. Reaching into her purse, Ms. Hammer produced a Colt .38 Detective's Special. When the car's driver spied the gun, he stopped the car, turned around, and peeled out of the garage. "Had I not had my gun," said the fifty-one-year-old woman, "I might not have lived to talk about it."

Case 3: The school day began like any other at Cleveland Elementary School in Stockton, California. But shortly before noontime, on 17 January 1989, a twenty-four-year-old drifter named Patrick Edward Purdy opened fire on the crowded schoolyard with a Chinese-made AK-47 assault rifle (purchased in Oregon) fitted with a "drum" magazine holding 75 bullets (purchased in Rhode Island). Purdy laid down a line of fire that killed five students and wounded thirty-three others. After firing 105 rounds, Purdy fired one final shot from a Taurus 9-mm semiautomatic pistol, killing himself on the spot. Purdy's motives were never entirely discovered, but investigators did find a history of drug and alcohol abuse, mental instability, brushes with the law, and a fascination with weapons of all kinds.

Case 4: In late 1997 and early 1998, a rash of schoolhouse shootings perpetrated by children and teenagers erupted around the country. On 14 March 1998, eleven-year-old Andrew Golden and thirteen-year-old Mitchell Johnson gathered several weapons from one of the boys' relatives and then stationed themselves on a hill overlooking the Westside Middle School in Jonesboro, Arkansas. One of the boys entered the school and pulled the school's fire alarm, prompting what everyone assumed was a fire drill. When the school had emptied, the two boys opened fire, killing four girls and a teacher. Ten students were injured. The boys were taken into custody along with an assortment of handguns and long guns, but the fatal gunfire came mostly from an M-1 carbine replica and a Remington .30-06 hunting rifle. A partial motive seemed to be that one of the boys had been spurned by a girl at the school.

Criminological Debate

As is true with public debate over the Second Amendment, most public debate and much policy discourse on the criminological consequences of guns is fragmentary in its treatment of fact, polemical in its tone, and narrow in its consideration of options. The four cases that begin this [viewpoint] typify some of the key criminological consequences of guns. They also exemplify the nature of public discourse on the gun issue, in that tragic incidents such as the Stockton and Jonesboro massacres receive considerable attention and therefore rivet public attention; moreover, the increase in such incidents in the past two decades has fanned reformist flames, supporting the call for stronger gun control, as well as for stiffer penalties for gun-related crimes.

While such incidents may serve the purposes of particular policymakers and interest groups, it is difficult to have confidence that good policy will result from a knee-jerk reaction to an unanticipated disaster. Yet this is a common pattern for the gun control issue. . . . To be sure, disasters have prompted desirable policy change in such areas as coal mine safety, automobile safety, and earthquake preparedness. In these and many other instances, necessary policy changes occurred only after significant human disasters. Yet it is difficult to have much confidence in a policy process that operates primarily through the outrage-action-reaction cycle.

The criminological debate assessed [here] is also politically significant for how the gun problem is defined. The "rights talk" surrounding the Second Amendment . . . is a political means used by control foes to blunt criminological analysis that supports stronger gun control. "Even if guns are harmful," the argument goes, "I have a right to own and lawfully use them as I see fit." Such an argument parallels others in which questionable behavior that might otherwise be controlled or prohibited is allowed because it falls under the Bill of Rights umbrella. For example, a wide array of hateful, hurtful, and otherwise objectionable speech is nevertheless protected by the courts because of the preeminent importance attached to the First Amendment's free speech protection. The Second Amendment does not fall into this same category, but its location in the Bill of Rights encourages gun control opponents to use "rights talk" to political advantage.

Arrayed against this view is a growing effort that emphasizes the gun problem as a public health issue. Spearheaded by public health and medical professionals, this effort dates to 1983, when the Centers for Disease Control (CDC) declared firearms violence to be a significant public health threat. That year, the CDC created a unit to gather and encourage research on gun-related violence, which in turn has spawned considerable public health and medical research (much of it discussed in this [viewpoint]) underscoring the public health threat posed by guns. President Reagan's surgeon general, C. Everett Koop, and President Clinton's first surgeon general, Joycelyn Elders, both weighed in strongly to push the public health definition of the problem. By tagging guns with the "public health threat" label and comparing them to such public health risks as smoking and automobile accidents, members of the medical community have sought to redefine the gun issue in order to alter public policy outcomes. It is a classic example of what the political scientist Murray Edelman has labeled symbolic politics—that is, shaping language and perception to political advantage: "The words a group employs and on which it relies . . . can often be taken as an index of group norms and conceptual frameworks." The concern expressed by the public health community became sufficiently threatening to gun control opponents that an effort was launched in 1995 by the National Rifle Association to get Congress to stop funding for CDC research on gun issues. (Firearms-related research by the CDC amounted to about $2.3 million a year.) That effort eventually succeeded.

Bearing in mind the role of language and symbols in the criminological debate over guns, the best way to assess the real consequences of guns in American life is to move beyond anecdote and outrage and examine instead the existing scholarship on the criminological consequences of guns. . . . So too must we examine whether the criminological consequences of guns pose obstacles or encouragement to gun control. It may be, for example, that the best available analysis points toward stricter regulation as a feasible means for stemming gun-related violence. Conversely, data and evidence may suggest that regulatory efforts are fruitless or even counterproductive. It may also be that existing analysis cannot offer any clear direction. No matter what the conclusion, it is impossible to understand the gun issue, and therefore its place in the larger policy framework, without consideration of this central issue. While the connections between guns and crime discussed here suggest a panoply of possible policy responses, this [viewpoint] focuses primarily on the general criminological picture. . . .

Maintaining public order and safety are primary, even primordial purposes of government. Regardless of one's view of guns, it is clear that firearms are intimately associated with a variety of disruptions of public order in American homes and on American streets. Thus, we begin with the nature of those disruptions.

America and Violence

America has long reigned supreme in levels of violence among the developed nations of the world. A Centers for Disease Control study of gun deaths worldwide in 1994 found that, among the thirty-six richest nations of the world,

22

Guns Are Used to Commit Crimes

Circumstances	Total murder victims	Total firearms	Handguns	Rifles	Shotguns	Other guns or type not stated	Knives or cutting instruments	Blunt objects (clubs, hammers, etc.)	Personal weapons (hands, fists, feet, etc.)	Poison	Pushed or thrown out window	Explosives	Fire	Narcotic
Rape	43	6	4	0	0	2	9	5	9	0	0	0	0	0
Robbery	1,092	797	664	24	34	75	93	74	47	0	0	0	3	
Burglary	96	56	45	2	6	3	18	10	5	0	0	0	0	
Larceny-theft	15	9	8	0	0	1	2	2	1	0	0	0	0	
Motor vehicle theft	16	9	4	2	1	2	2	0	0	0	0	1	0	
Arson	59	3	3	0	0	0	0	0	1	0	0	4	35	
Prostitution and commercialized vice	8	1	1	0	0	0	2	2	0	0	0	0	0	
Other sex offenses	8	0	0	0	0	0	1	1	5	0	0	0	0	
Narcotic drug laws	657	553	425	22	14	92	39	13	11	0	1	0	2	1
Gambling	5	5	5	0	0	0	0	0	0	0	0	0	0	
Other— not specified	315	201	145	13	9	34	32	9	20	1	0	0	4	

"Murder Circumstances," Federal Bureau of Investigation, 2003.

the United States had by far the highest rate of gun deaths (combining homicide, suicide, and accident), amounting to 14.24 per 100,000 people. Of 88,649 gun deaths reported by these countries, 45 percent occurred in the United States. The United States has a far higher firearm death rate than other developed nations, and it has a higher ratio of gun homicides and gun suicides.

The gulf between the United States and other nations was dramatized by an incident that occurred on Halloween night in 1992, when a Japanese exchange student was shot and killed at a home near Baton Rouge, Louisiana. The student, sixteen-year-old Yoshihiro Hattori, was looking for a Halloween party in the neighborhood of Rodney Peairs when he mistakenly approached the Peairs door. As the student (costumed as John Travolta from the movie *Saturday Night Fever*) and a friend approached the door, Mrs. Peairs yelled to her husband to get his gun, apparently believing the two to be assailants. When the students entered the family's carport, Mr. Peairs ordered them to "freeze." When Hattori continued to advance toward the man, Peairs shot the student once with a .44 Magnum revolver. Peairs was tried for manslaughter in 1993 but was acquitted on the grounds that he believed the threat to be legitimate (the student carried a camera in his hand, which Peairs took to be some kind of weapon). It turned out that Hattori spoke little English and probably considered Peairs's actions to be consistent with Halloween traditions.

The man's acquittal sent shock waves throughout Japan, which had followed the trial closely. One Japanese professor, an expert on American studies, said, "We are more civilized. We rely on words." The incident "seemed to confirm the Japanese view of America as a place rife with guns." A major Japanese newspaper said that the town where the student was killed "is like an old-frontier town of the old wild west." To the Japanese, the killing and its justification were almost beyond understanding and seemed to confirm the belief that America was a nation of lawless, gun-toting vigilantes. The parents of the dead student did prevail in a civil action, winning $650,000 in damages in September 1994. The judge observed that "there was absolutely no need for the resort to a dangerous weapon."

In image as well as in fact, guns are closely linked to American patterns of violence. The homicide rate began to rise dramatically in the 1960s, as did the production and sale of handguns. Two-thirds of homicides and three-fifths of suicides are committed with guns, as are one-third of robberies and one-fifth of aggravated assaults. In all, guns are used in more than one million violent crimes each year.

Americans are by no means unmindful of gun and violence problems. Concerns about crime, violence, and law and order have been important political issues for decades. In 1968, Richard Nixon won the presidency on a tough law-and-order platform that resonated with voters concerned about crime and lawlessness. With some fluctuations, the issue has continued to be potent from the national to the local level, with a notable upswing in 1993 and 1994, when crime and violence were considered the second most important problem facing the country, exceeded only by the economy and jobs.

In every year since 1972, guns have accounted for more than 30,000 deaths annually. Yet for nearly all those years, more gun deaths are attributable to suicide than to homicide. In 1991, for example, of the 38,317 reported gun deaths, 18,350 were homicides, but 18,526 were suicides. The remainder, 1,441, were accidental deaths. In 1994, gun deaths totaled 39,720, including 20,540 suicides and 13,593 homicides. In 1995, there were 18,503 gun suicides, 15,853 gun homicides, 1,225 accidental gun deaths, and 394 deaths from undetermined gun-related causes, totaling 35,957 Americans who died from firearms. In 1998, records show that 30,708 gun deaths occurred, including 17,424 suicides, 11,798 homicides, 866 fatal accidents, and 620 other gun-related deaths. By way of comparison, the FBI reported 167 justifiable gun homicides by civilians in 1998. This ratio of homicides to suicides is especially significant from a policy standpoint because the primary, almost exclusive, focus of public and governmental attention has been the crime problem. . . .

Gauging Loss of Life

One way to gauge this loss of life is to compare it to other circumstances when Americans have died in large numbers.

For example, about 42,000 people were killed in highway accidents in 1997, compared with 32,436 firearms deaths the same year (although the auto fatality figure has been declining in recent years because of increased auto safety and a decline in drunk driving). Roughly 400,000 Americans were killed in World War II. About 60,000 were killed in the Vietnam War.

In demographic terms, gun homicides do not affect the population uniformly but occur disproportionately among youths, males, and African Americans. These three groups in particular have experienced a rapid rise in gun deaths. Between 1979 and 1991, 24,552 children and adolescents were gun homicide victims, 16,614 committed suicide with guns, and 7,257 were killed in gun accidents. In 1993, 5,751 people under the age of twenty died from guns. This figure includes 3,661 homicides, 1,460 suicides, 526 accidents, and 104 deaths from undetermined causes. These data were compiled by the Children's Defense Fund, drawn from the National Center for Health Statistics. For the fifteen to nineteen age group, the fatality rate from automobile accidents (the leading cause of death) was 44 per 100,000 people in 1979; by 1989, that rate had fallen to 34 per 100,000. But in the same time span, homicide and suicide gun deaths rose among the same age group from 12 per 100,000 to 18. Among black males ages fifteen to nineteen, the gun death rate rose from 37 per 100,000 in 1985 to an alarming 105 in 1990. From 1985 to 1993, the number of homicides of male African Americans ages thirteen to seventeen tripled. In the early 1990s, homicide rates of African American males in their early twenties were more than eight times as high as those for males as a whole. While overall gun deaths declined on a per capita basis in the 1990s, these demographic groups continued to be most susceptible to gun violence. According to a 1999 U.S. Department of Justice report, "firearms play a large role in juvenile violence," reflected in the facts that firearms played a role in more than 80 percent of juvenile violence incidents discussed in the report, and accounted for 83 percent of juvenile homicides in Milwaukee, 85 percent of juvenile homicides in the District of Columbia, and 91 percent of such homicides in Los Angeles. Further, these changes have occurred at a time when the proportion of young people as a percentage of the total population has actually been declining. According to criminal justice expert Scott Decker, the "decreasing age of both offenders and victims is the most profound change in homicide rates since World War II." According to one police figure, the explanation is "population [shifts], gangs and easy accessibility of weapons." A 2000 government report noted that the sharp increase in juvenile homicides from the mid-1980s through the early 1990s, and the subsequent drop in such homicides in the late 1990s, were both "firearm-related" and "linked to gun use."

In addition to gun deaths, a far larger number of people are injured by guns each year, whether by intention or by accident. For every gun death, there are an estimated five to seven gun injuries. Despite the vagueness of this figure, it is generally accepted. (The vagueness of this ratio is attributable to the fact that data on gun-related injuries are not systematically kept on a national scale.) The public policy and public health consequences of gun injuries are substantial: the annual national cost of intentional and unintentional gun injuries was estimated in 1993 to be more than $14 billion per year, with most of those costs covered directly or indirectly by public monies. Direct costs to hospitals were about $1 billion. According to policy analysts Philip J. Cook and Jens Ludwig, the total yearly costs of all gun violence nationwide, taking into account the full range of costs borne by society including health care, security, prevention efforts, familial consequences, and other factors, are a staggering $100 billion.

Some consider these death and injury figures sufficient, in and of themselves, to justify much more stringent gun control laws. Others argue that they simply represent the inevitable by-product of a modern, complex society that is also armed, and for which the justification for having guns outweighs these negative consequences.

"The emphasis on firearms availability . . . provides a convenient distraction for those analysts who prefer to avoid addressing some very distressing questions about the nature of our society and ourselves."

The Extent of Gun Violence Is Exaggerated

James B. Jacobs

In the following viewpoint James B. Jacobs challenges the claim that violent crime is caused by the widespread availability of guns. He concedes that America is an exceedingly violent nation but argues that the vast majority of violent crimes are committed without a weapon. He also contends that as gun ownership has increased, gun violence has decreased. Jacobs is the director of the Center for Research in Crime and Justice at New York University as well as the Chief Justice Warren E. Burger Professor of Constitutional Law and the Courts.

As you read, consider the following questions:
1. Why does the author say that analysts should not jump to the conclusion that America's violent crime problem is a consequence of the availability of guns?
2. What factors does the author use to explain the American predilection for violence?
3. What do recent studies say about the self-defensive uses of firearms, according to Jacobs?

James B. Jacobs, *Can Gun Control Work?* New York: Oxford University Press. Copyright © 2002 by Oxford University Press, Inc. Reproduced by permission.

Recently, much attention in the gun control debate has focused on mandatory trigger locks and safe storage. Gun controls like these are aimed at preventing firearms accidents rather than gun crime or suicide. Indeed, gun control proponents frequently emphasize that the household firearm poses a risk to its occupants, especially children. Thus, many readers will be surprised to learn that in 1997, only 40 children under age 5 were killed in firearms accidents. That same year, 600 children under 5 died in drowning accidents and 1,100 died in motor vehicle accidents. Likewise, the numbers of fatal accidents involving children under 15 included 1,050 drownings, 3,100 motor vehicle deaths, and 220 firearms deaths.

All accidental deaths and serious injuries are tragic, and we ought to strive to prevent as many as possible. Still, firearms accidents are not a leading cause of accidental deaths for Americans. Consider that in 1997 there were approximately 93,800 accidental deaths from all causes; of these, motor vehicle accidents accounted for 43,200, falls for 14,900, drownings for 4,000, and firearms for 1,500. Moreover the number of unintentional deaths inflicted by firearms has declined steadily for the past several decades, despite increases in the nation's population and in the number of firearms in private hands.

Suicide

In 1979, there were 27,200 suicides; twenty years later there were 30,500. Approximately 57% of the suicides in both years were carried out by means of firearms. Does the fact that the percentage of suicides committed with firearms is much higher in the United States than in other countries mean that suicide, like homicide, ought to be thought of as a by-product of America's firearms policy? I think not. If there were a strong causal relationship between firearms and suicide, the United States would be a world leader in suicide as it is in homicide. But this is not the case. Unlike the U.S. homicide rate, the U.S. suicide rate is average for industrialized nations. The suicide rate for the United States in 1996 was 11.6 per 100,000. Comparable figures for some other countries are: United Kingdom 7.7; Canada 13.2; Germany

15.6; Japan 16.7; France 20.8; and Finland 27.2. Many countries have much higher suicide rates than the United States; indeed, a number of countries have so much suicide that they have a higher *combined* suicide and homicide rate than the United States. While it is possible that some people commit suicide on impulse because a firearm is available, I think it more likely that Americans decide on suicide for the same reasons that people in other countries do. However, in deciding how to commit suicide, Americans frequently utilize firearms, a readily available and highly effective means.

Admittedly, Ronald Clarke's and Pat Mayhew's famous study of coal gas in the United Kingdom warns us not to dismiss the instrumentality hypothesis too quickly. They found that suicide dropped significantly when coal gas, a preferred method of suicide, was replaced by natural gas. Clarke and Mayhew conclude that the ready availability of an effective means of suicide led some people to commit suicide who otherwise would not. But the data are subject to varying interpretations. In 2000, [David] Gunnell et al. found that while there was indeed a 34% decrease in suicide by gas (for men), there was a 29% increase in suicide by drug overdose. Women experienced an 89% decrease in suicide by gas, but a 305% increase in suicide by drugs.

It would be a mistake to see suicide as primarily or substantially a "gun problem." It is hardly obvious that suicide would be substantially reduced, or reduced at all, if firearms were less available, as is the case in many countries with higher suicide rates. But, for purposes of this [viewpoint], that question is beside the point. We will focus on whether there are any realistic strategies that could reduce access to firearms by persons at risk of suicide.

Multiple Killings and Rampage Killers

Multiple killings (more than two victims in a single episode) must be considered part of the gun problem. If guns didn't exist, we probably would not have suffered the December 7, 1993, massacre on the Long Island Railroad, the April 1999 Columbine school shooting, and other multiple homicides. Although firearms make mass killings possible, the 1993 World Trade Center bombing and the 1995 Oklahoma City bombing are two poignant reminders that guns are not the only way that madmen and terrorists can inflict mass destruction. (Just as I was putting the finishing touches to this . . . in September 2001, two incidents of mass murder in California and Iowa were perpetrated with knives. Then on September 11, 2001, terrorists using knives seized four commercial airlines and crashed them into the World Trade Center, the Pentagon, and a field in Pennsylvania, killing 3,000 persons.) Fortunately, and perhaps surprisingly in light of the massive publicity they attract, multiple killings remain very rare in American society. Moreover, while the number of guns has been increasing steadily, the number of mass killings has remained fairly constant.

Homicidal rampages at school naturally and justifiably attract enormous media attention, but it is important to examine these events realistically. Since 1992, when the U.S. Centers for Disease Control (CDC) began tracking school violence, shooting deaths at school have declined every year. The 40 school shooting deaths in the 1997–1998 school year were within the midrange of the annual toll since 1992. According to the National School Safety Center, violent deaths in school settings (suicides and homicides) declined 27.3% between the 1992–1993 and the 1997–1998 school years. In the 2000–2001 school year, the number of homicides and suicides in schools was 41% of its 1992–1993 level. . . .

Firearms are a necessary, but obviously insufficient, explanation for most mass killings. Obviously, the killer's mental condition is crucially important. In retrospect, many mass killers and the majority of recent school shooters gave indications or told others of an impending rampage. True, *if* these unstable people could be prevented from obtaining firearms, they might not be able to carry out their demented plans (unless they used explosives), but this is a big *if*, given the very small number of events. (Moreover, federal law makes it a felony to knowingly sell or give a handgun to a person under 21 years old or a long gun to a person under 18.) Homicidal rampages should also direct attention to the school environment itself. Are our schools too large and anonymous? Is bullying allowed to go on unchallenged? Does depression and humiliation regularly go unrecognized and unaddressed? Concern about the availability of guns ought not to overwhelm questions like these.

Guns and Crime

What makes gun control such a compelling priority for many opinion leaders and a large segment of the population is the belief that violent crime is caused by the widespread availability of firearms and could be reduced by eliminating or limiting firearms availability.

There can be no denying that the United States has a serious *violent crime* problem. Frank Zimring and Gordon Hawkins have shown that U.S. property crime rates do not differ much from Britain's or Australia's, while the violent crime rate is vastly higher. In 1998, there were approximately 9,100 firearms homicides (and 14,088 total homicides) in the United States, while there were less than 50 firearms homicides (750 total) in Britain, which has ⅕ as great a population. Ought we to infer that it is the availability of firearms (especially handguns) to private citizens that is responsible for America's immensely higher rate?

It would be a mistake to jump to that conclusion. The United States has much more violent crime, with and without firearms, than the other Western democracies. Our rape, robbery, and aggravated assault rates are much higher than those in other countries. But only a small fraction of those crimes are committed with guns; more than 90% of violent crimes are committed *without any weapon whatsoever.* Thus, we ought not to jump to the conclusion that America's violent crime problem is fully, essentially, or even substantially a consequence of the legal availability of firearms.

A close look at U.S. homicide data confirms that there must be more to the very high U.S. violent crime rate than just the large percentage of citizens who own firearms or the easy availability of firearms to private citizens. Homicides, much less robberies, do not occur randomly across all segments of the population. The majority of homicide perpetrators have criminal records as do the majority of the victims. In other words, lethal violence occurs disproportionately within a criminal subculture, and in the last two decades especially among people involved in the drug trade.

Guns Are Not Always the Weapon of Choice

Presence of offender's weapon	Violent crime		Rape/sexual assaults		Robbery		Simple and aggravated assault	
	Number	Percent	Number	Percent	Number	Percent	Number	Percent
Total	4,949,380	100%	191,350	100%	552,830	100%	4,205,190	100%
No weapon	3,398,040	69%	160,960	84%	223,620	41%	3,013,450	72%
Weapon	1,166,570	24%	20,690	11%*	246,280	45%	899,070	21%
Firearm	366,840	7	5,860	3 *	138,280	25	222,700	5
Knife	331,240	7	11,380	6 *	56,570	10	263,290	6
Other	427,510	9	3,450	2 *	41,840	8	382,220	9
Type not ascertained	40,980	1	0	0 *	10,120	2 *	30,860	1 *
Don't know	384,770	8%	9,710	5%*	82,390	15%	292,670	7%

*Based on 10 or fewer sample cases.

Note: Percentages may not total to 100% because of rounding. If the offender was armed with more than one weapon, the crime is classified based on the most serious weapon present.

"Presence of Weapons in Violent Incidents, 2003," *Criminal Victimization, 2003*, Bureau of Justice Statistics, National Crime Victimization Service, Department of Justice, September 2004.

Undoubtedly, there are many factors that explain Americans' predilection for violence with and without guns: for example, the legacy of slavery and racial oppression, frontier tradition, vast income inequalities, a southern code of honor, terrible pockets of poverty, and weak community controls. There are huge literatures in history, psychology, sociology, and economics, attempting to account for violence in America.

[Studies] show that African-Americans are the victims of homicide six times more often than European-Americans, and that they are the perpetrators of homicide seven times more often than European-Americans. Any satisfactory explanation of lethal violence would have to take account of the socioeconomic predicament and cultural norms of communities and neighborhoods with disproportionately high rates of violence. Perhaps the emphasis on firearms availability (and drugs) provides a convenient distraction for those analysts who prefer to avoid addressing some very distressing questions about the nature of our society and ourselves.

Using international statistics, Gary Kleck has shown that the violent crime rate is not a function of gun availability; removing the United States from an analysis of international rates of gun ownership and homicide practically erases the correlation. Some countries have high rates of firearms ownership (Switzerland and Israel) and low rates of violent crime. Likewise, some countries (e.g., Mexico) have low rates of private gun ownership (at least according to official data) and high rates of violent crime. Moreover, in the United States, there is no significant correlation between rates of firearm ownership and rates of firearm homicide at the state or city levels. In other words, knowing the percentage of people in an American state or city who own firearms is of no help in predicting the firearm homicide rate in that state or city.

Perhaps adding to the puzzlement is the fact that while the stock of firearms in private hands has grown steadily during this century, the rate of violent crime has fluctuated. The United States experienced an extraordinary increase in violent crime in the 1960s and 1970s and a remarkable drop in violent crime in the 1990s. The number of firearms, especially handguns, in private hands increased by several million every year during this period. The relentless growth in the privately held stock of firearms cannot explain both the crime wave of the first period and the crime drop of the second period.

There is a good deal of research and scholarly debate on whether, even if guns don't cause crime, they cause greater likelihood of injury or death when they are used in crime. This is also a complex issue to resolve empirically. Interestingly, although not surprisingly, robbers with guns less frequently cause any injury than robbers with knives; they get more victim compliance. But when bullets are fired and hit a human target, they do greater damage than knife wounds. Still, the differential damage might not be solely due to a gun effect; those who use guns may intend the most serious injuries. If so, even if they were somehow denied a gun, they might inflict grievous or deadly injury with a knife, tire iron, or their bare hands. . . .

The Value of Firearms

We cannot properly assess the nature and magnitude of the gun problem without considering the offsetting benefits of guns. Many gun control proponents assert that guns, especially handguns, provide no benefits whatsoever, and that individuals who believe that guns make them safer are wrong, perhaps suffering from a species of false consciousness. Relying heavily on suicide statistics, they purport to show that owning a gun is more likely to lead to death or injury of the owner or someone in his family than to the death or injury of an intruder or attacker. The following excerpt is typical:

> The home can be a dangerous place. We noted 43 suicides, criminal homicides, or accidental gunshot deaths involving a gun kept in the home for every case of homicide for self-protection. In the light of these findings, it may reasonably be asked whether keeping firearms in the home increases a family's protection or places it in greater danger.

Gun rights advocates counter that the number of criminals killed or injured by citizens using their firearms in self-defense is not the right measure of the self-defensive value of firearms. A homeowner can ward off an intruder, rapist, robber, or mugger without anybody being injured, indeed, without firing shots. Using a survey, criminologist Gary Kleck found that Americans defend themselves 2.5 million times per year by warding off threats to their persons and property. Phil

Cook and Jens Ludwig put the number of defensive gun uses at 1.3 million per year. [David] Hemenway and [Deborah] Azrael's national survey, sponsored by the National Institute of Justice, found 1.5 million defensive gun uses per year. All these surveys reveal a great deal of self-defensive use of firearms, in fact, more defensive gun uses than crimes committed with firearms. (For 1999, the National Crime Victimization Survey estimated approximately 563,000 crimes committed with a gun; for 1997, the FBI's Uniform Crime Reports reported 425,000 firearm-related violent crimes.)

In addition to the number of defensive gun uses, gun owners maintain that guns provide a social benefit via the subjective sense of security that gun owners derive from having their guns available. This makes sense. We recognize life insurance as providing a social benefit, even if the policy owner doesn't die; the value lies in the psychic protection it affords to the policyholder and his or her family. Likewise, automobile owners derive enormous psychic satisfaction from possessing and operating the automobile, even if it subjects them to risk of accident and death and is less efficient than public transportation. Gun ownership could be analogized to investments in door and window locks. Are such security devices valueless until they successfully prevent an intrusion? Clearly, security devices provide psychic security to the homeowner, even if never tested by an intruder.

In assessing the benefits and costs of firearms, it is senseless to lump all firearms together. Rifles and shotguns are infrequently used in crimes but widely used in hunting and competitive and recreational shooting. There would seem to be no basis for dismissing or discounting the individual and social benefits of hunting, target shooting, and gun collecting. People engage in many sports and activities that pose some risk to themselves, and, in some cases, to others. While rifles and shotguns can also provide self-defense, lightweight handguns are especially useful for this purpose. Handguns are not used as much in hunting, but there are some hunters who use them. Some handguns are used in competitive shooting and recreationally. Most handguns are purchased for self-defense. Most handguns owners claim to derive a feeling of security from being armed.

"The bottom line is that American children are at high risk of getting shot."

Youth Gun Violence Is a Serious Problem

Josh Sugarmann

Josh Sugarmann claims in the following viewpoint that firearms are the second leading cause of death among teenagers. He contends that youths have no difficulty in obtaining guns, and carry them for protection or to intimidate others. Sugarmann also argues that pro-gun groups try to get children interested in guns in order to create future members for their organizations. Josh Sugarmann is executive director of the Violence Policy Center and author of *Every Handgun Is Aimed at You*, the source of this viewpoint.

As you read, consider the following questions:
1. How much higher are the firearms homicide and suicide rates for American kids in comparison to kids in other industrialized nations, according to the author?
2. According to a 1996 survey by the National Institute of Justice, why do youths carry guns?
3. In the author's view, how is the National Rifle Association and other pro-gun groups creating a youth market for guns?

The number of children unintentionally shot and killed each year in the United States could fill a commercial airliner. In 1997 alone, 142 kids 14 years of age or younger were killed by firearms unintentionally—12 children every month or one child every two and a half days. More than 10 times that number of children are treated in U.S. emergency rooms each year for non-fatal gunshot wounds, many resulting in permanent injury and disfigurement.

Child Gun Deaths

Evening newscasts and daily newspapers regularly recount how children kill themselves or their playmates with handguns. Public health research has found that unintentional shootings occur most frequently inside the home. The most common scenario is a child playing with a gun that was stored out of view, but loaded and unlocked. Some examples include:

- From the January 15, 1996, *Fort Myers News-Press*— Two-year-old Kaile Hinke was shot in the chest by her three-year-old brother, Colton. Colton found the loaded .25-caliber pistol in a drawer in his parents' bedroom, where he and Kaile were playing while their mother was in another room. Kaile was driven to Lee Memorial Hospital where she was pronounced dead.
- From the February 18, 1996, *Salt Lake Tribune*— Thirteen-year-old LeRoy Paul was shot in the throat by his 12-year-old best friend. Police believe the young shooter, who thought the pistol was not loaded, had chambered a round that remained in the Ruger 9mm after the magazine was removed. Paul was flown to Primary Children's Hospital where he was pronounced dead.
- From the March 22, 1996, Stockton, California, *Record* —Nineteen-month-old Omar Sanad was shot in the face by his 12-year-old brother. The older brother found the .380-caliber handgun inside his parents' bedroom. He brought it outside and was waving it around, while pulling his toddler brother in a plastic sled, when it discharged. Omar was transported by Med Flight to Sutter Amador Hospital where he was pronounced dead.

After motor vehicles, firearms are the second leading cause of death among all teenagers. The effects of gun violence on American children becomes starkly apparent when international comparisons are made. A 1997 study published in *Morbidity and Mortality Weekly Report* analyzed firearm deaths for children aged 14 or younger in 26 industrialized countries and found that 86 percent of the deaths occurred in the United States. The firearms homicide rate alone was 16 times higher for American children; the firearms suicide rate 11 times higher; and the firearms unintentional death rate nine times higher.

Borgman. © 1995 by the *Cincinnati Enquirer*. Reproduced by permission.

Not surprisingly, at the same time that firearms violence among youth has increased, so has gun carrying. In explaining why, youth often echo the rationalization of their elders: self-defense. A 1996 nationwide survey by the National Institute of Justice of high school students found that, of those respondents who admitted to carrying a gun, 43 percent cited protection from violence in their neighborhoods. Nonetheless, an alarming 36 percent admitted to carrying a gun in order to "scare someone" or "get back at someone."

While studies show that urban gang membership is a predictor of handgun carrying, the same studies reveal an increase in white suburban adolescent gun carrying—up 130 percent over the course of a decade. Also, gun carrying is more prevalent in smaller communities. More disturbingly, the National Institute of Justice survey found that when a gun was carried outside the home by a high school–aged youth, it was most likely a semiautomatic handgun (50 percent) and next most likely a revolver (30 percent). Where are these kids getting the guns? Most looked no further than their own homes. Of the students surveyed, 52 percent indicated they had been given or loaned a gun by a family member or had taken it from their home without their parents' permission.

Youth and guns have come to be equated in the public's mind with the school shootings that have dominated the news over the past three years [prior to 2001]. The common thread in these cases was the presence of handguns in the shooters' possession at the time of their arrests, and the evidence that the majority had used them to attack their classmates. School shootings are the most grotesque manifestation of youth gun violence, but they are no more representative than unintentional shootings. The vast majority of youth gun deaths are day-in-and-day-out, run-of-the-mill homicides and suicides, usually involving handguns. For America's children and teens, a Columbine occurs every day—except that the killing is spread across the entire nation.

American Children Are in Danger

The bottom line is that American children are at high risk of getting shot. Have American children been molded by the mass media to be more violent than kids in other nations? There exists today a global youth culture featuring considerable violence and dominated by the American entertainment media. Yet children in other industrialized countries have vastly lower rates of firearms death and injury. Regarding the effects of electronic media, Japanese children are exposed to video games even more violent than those found in America, yet they almost never kill each other. The argument can be made that American children are at a higher risk of getting shot, *not* because they are warped by our culture into little killing machines, but because American children have easier access to the supreme killing machine itself—the handgun. To help reduce the youth firearms death rate, the American Academy of Pediatrics (AAP) advocates an agenda of "passive

Firearm Access

The Youth Handgun Safety Act of 1994 prohibits possession of handguns by anyone under the age of 18, and under
the Gun Control Act of 1968 it is unlawful for federally licensed firearms dealers to sell handguns to persons under
21. Yet, youth appear to have little difficulty in obtaining
handguns. In one survey of 7th and 10th graders in Milwaukee and Boston, 42% reported that they could get a gun if
they wanted one, and 28% reported having handled a gun
without adult knowledge or supervision. How do teenagers
acquire guns? When juvenile offenders in detention centers
were interviewed about how they acquired their first gun,
42% indicated that they were given their first gun by a peer,
an older youth, or a relative, while 38% purposefully acquired their first gun by borrowing (17%), buying (11%),
or stealing (10%). 84% of those who possessed guns said
that they had obtained them before they were 15 years old.

Many youth have access to guns in their homes. A recent
study found that 43% of households in the U.S. with children under 18 had at least one gun. 21% of gun owners with
children under 18 reported that they stored their weapons
loaded, and 9% reported that their weapons were stored
loaded and unlocked. A study looking at the source of
weapons involved in self-inflicted and unintentional injuries
among youth found that parents owned the guns used in
more than half (57%) of the suicides and suicide attempts
and in almost one in five (19%) unintentional injuries and
deaths by adolescents ages 19 and younger. 90% of guns
used in suicide attempts and three-quarters (72%) of guns
involved in unintentional injuries were stored in the home
of the victim, a relative, or a friend.

"Youth Firearm-Related Violence Fact Sheet," National Youth Violence
Prevention Resource Center, 2005.

protection" for our young people, which includes support for:
- The "absence of guns from homes and communities";
- Subjecting guns to safety and design regulations, like
  other consumer products; and
- Firearm regulation, including bans of handguns and as-
  sault weapons.

While the AAP and other child-care experts have no problem making a direct correlation between handgun availability
and the threat posed to youth by gun violence, the firearms
industry and their supporters hold a far different view.

A Battle for Their Hearts and Minds

The National Rifle Association and the gun industry have come up with a "solution" to the problem of kids and guns that, although startling to some, is actually quite predictable: *what the kids need are more guns!* They contend that an early familiarity with firearms, culminating in ownership, is the foundaion of patriotism and civic virtue. Left unsaid to the general public, but repeated in the pages of gun industry and pro-gun publications, is that involving youth in the gun culture is essential to maintaining both the political might of the NRA [National Rifle Association] and the financial health of the firearms industry. For this reason, NRA Executive Vice President Wayne LaPierre declared in the March 2000 issue of the NRA's *American Guardian* magazine:

> The battle over gun control is no longer about crime and criminals. The battle is about kids—our kids—stepping into an America dominated by the anti-gun media and politicians.

Learning a lesson from the tobacco industry, gunmakers recognize that new customers must be enticed before they reach adulthood. Participation in shooting activities must begin at an early age: according to a study published by the Fish and Wildlife Reference Service, men and women who do not become hunters by the time they graduate from high school are unlikely to ever do so. A "strategic analysis" for the firearms industry concluded that "there is a continuing need to encourage new first-time shooters and, as much as is practical and responsible, ease their entry into the shooting sports."

Having in their own words already "lost a generation" to video games, coupled with a general decline in interest in the shooting sports, the NRA has joined with the gun industry to create a new youth gun culture. At the NRA's 1996 Annual Meeting, Marion Hammer, the NRA's first woman president, introduced her 10-year-old grandson to the assembled membership, stating, "I know that when NRA reaches out and takes the hand of a child, we are touching America's future." Hammer outlined the NRA's agenda to "invest" in America's youth:

> I pledge to you to dedicate my term in office to two demanding missions. One is building an NRA bridge to America's youth. The other is being fiscally far-sighted to provide for

bold new programs that will teach America's children values to last a lifetime. It will be an old-fashioned wrestling match for the hearts and minds of our children, and we'd better engage our adversaries with no holds barred. . . . If we do not successfully reach out to the next generation, then the freedom and liberty that we've lived for—and that many of our ancestors have died for—will not live beyond us.

In 1997, Hammer's eventual successor as NRA president; actor Charlton Heston, announced in the organization's *American Rifleman* magazine a planned $100 million campaign, of which a key focus would be no re-engage the NRA's "lost generation." In September's "very special issue" of the magazine, dedicated to saving the Second Amendment throughout the mobilization of children, Heston warned:

> Many modern youth think the right to keep and bear arms, the Second Amendment to the Constitution, seems sinister, even criminal. . . . I am back [in the public arena] because I see a nation of children, a couple of entire generations, that have been brainwashed into believing that the Second Amendment is criminal in origin, rather than framed within the Constitution.

Heston promised to deliver to his readers, within three years, a pro–Second Amendment president in the White House, a pro–Second Amendment Congress, and "most of all, a pro–Second Amendment generation of young people. . . ."

The NRA youth publication *InSights*—for junior NRA members aged 17 and under—routinely carries ads for firearms, including handguns like the Harrington & Richardson 929 Sidekick revolver. A May 1997 cover story, "Pistols on the Firing Line," displayed a variety of .22-caliber target pistols, many of which mimicked in design their higher-caliber cousins used on city streets. Most Americans would question putting a handgun into a child's hand, but NRA Executive Vice President Wayne LaPierre is unconcerned. His magazine column proclaims: "Gun ownership is intrinsically good and intrinsically innocent." The NRA's efforts have not gone unnoticed by the gun industry. In an article in *Fishing & Hunting News*, ammunition and reloading component manufacturer Frank Brownell enthused: "You always have to bring young people into anything. New blood really helps. . . . The NRA is . . . plowing new ground for this industry."

"The politician-media-institution campaign on 'youth violence' is bigoted and devoid of genuine concern for youths."

The Problem of Youth Gun Violence Is Exaggerated

Mike Males

According to Mike Males in the following viewpoint, the media portray the extent and severity of youth gun violence as far greater than it really is. In particular, the news media exaggerate the problem of school violence, suggesting that school shootings occur much more often than they do, he claims. In fact, such events are rare, and youths are actually safer in schools than they are at home, in the streets, or at work, Males argues. Those responsible for the vast majority of violent crime in the United States are adults, he contends. Mike Males is a sociologist and the author of several books on adolescents.

As you read, consider the following questions:
1. What percentage of teachers rated their schools as safe, according to a 1997 *Los Angeles Times* survey?
2. According to Males, why were thirty-nine school murders neglected by the media?
3. What is the typical profile of a rampage shooter, as reported by the author?

Monitoring the Future, an annual survey of 12,500 high school seniors by the University of Michigan's Institute for Social Research, is one of America's most widely quoted surveys on youth behavior. Its release every December provokes a media and official frenzy over student drug use. Curiously, one of the survey's most interesting findings relevant to one of this era's biggest fears is never quoted: its findings regarding school violence trends.

Despite their worshipful citation in press and official forums, self-reporting surveys are weak, highly suspect research tools. However, *Monitoring* is the only long-term consistently-administered survey of school violence available, and its trends follow the crime cycles in larger society. Its finding that both white and black students report less weapons-related victimization in school today than in the 1970s is consistent with other self-reported violence (students also report fewer instances of being deliberately injured by persons without weapons, being threatened with weapons, or being threatened with any kind of violence at school). The stable, generally declining pattern of violence among white students and the higher, cyclical pattern among black students is consistent with FBI crime reports.

Children Are Safer at School

In 2000, 3% of black high school seniors report being injured by someone with a weapon at school, on the way to or from school, or at a school event sometime in the year—down from 4% in 1999 and the lowest percentage in the survey's 24-year history. If that makes schools seem pretty dangerous, reflect on these even more unsettling perspectives: school safety and crime reports show only one-sixth of 1% of the nation's murders occur in schools, and hospital emergency department records analyzed by the U.S. Bureau of Justice Statistics found homes, workplaces, and streets account for eight, five, and 2.5 times more violence-related injuries, respectively, than do schools.

School and police agencies report the rate of injury with weapons in senior high schools is 46 per 100,000 students, and while they don't learn about most assaults, serious injuries would not escape notice. American schools are the site of a good deal of violence, but apparently not as much as other institutions, led by the family. Thus, statements that students are safer from murder and serious injury at school than at home, in the streets, or at work are factual but not necessarily comforting. The only comforting aspect is that most school violence is apparently low-level.

The *Monitoring* findings also directly contradict anecdotal quotes in the press from school personnel, experts, and teen-book authors that today's students are far more violent than those of past generations. These anecdotal quotes also appear at odds with what most teachers report. A 1997 *Los Angeles Times* survey of 545 students, 1,100 teachers, and 2,600 parents and other adults that found that 91% of students and 92% of teachers in Los Angeles (supposedly America's arch-drug/gang/gunplay capital) rated their schools as "safe." Only 14% of students had ever been in a fight at school, and only 1% had been in a fight involving a weapon.

However, adults not involved with public schools as teachers or parents—that is, ones whose impressions derive from media images and quotable authorities—were six to 10 times more likely to rate schools as imperiled by gangs, violence, and drugs than were the teachers and students inhabiting those schools. *Times* editors (the same ones who editorially lament lack of public support for school funding) apparently thought the public was insufficiently terrified of public schools. . . .

That there is some violence in public schools—led by the school shootings of 1997–2001 that received gargantuan media attention—properly draws concern, outrage, even (in cases such as the Columbine High School slaughter) horror. But there is no excuse for Americans being surprised that schools are not violence-free. The lack of perspective was pointed out by Justice Policy Institute president Vincent Schiraldi in a November 22, 1999, commentary in the *Los Angeles Times:*

> Nowadays, it is impossible to talk about juvenile crime and not discuss school shootings. Yet school shootings are extremely rare and not on the increase. In a population of about 50 million schoolchildren, there were approximately 55 school-associated violent deaths in the 1992–93 school year and fewer than half that in the 1998–99 school year. By comparison, in 1997, 88 people were killed by lightning—what

might be considered the gold standard for idiosyncratic events. Children who are killed in the United States are almost never killed inside a school. Yes, 12 kids were killed at Columbine. But by comparison, every two days in the U.S., 11 children die at the hands of their parents or guardians.

Bigotry

The term "youth violence," a media and official staple, is inherently prejudicial. To understand this, consider how we treat other demographic groups. Example: About one million Orthodox Jews live in the United States. Crime statistics aren't kept by creed, but assume a half-dozen commit murder every year.

This would give Orthodox Jews one of the lowest homicide rates of any group—probably the case. That means that every two months, on average, an Orthodox Jew is arrested for murder. Let's further assume that powerful political demagogues want to depict Jews as the font of violence, and the major media and institutions, as always, go along. Every couple of months, then, the press erupts, headlining "another Jew violence" tragedy, with sensational pictures and overwrought speculation as to "why Jews are so violent." The press and politicians resolutely ignore thousands of intervening murders by non-Jews, including murders of Jews by Gentiles, while connecting every Jewish homicide, no matter how occasional, into a "spate of Jew killings." Conservatives angrily demand tougher policing of Jews. Liberals blame violent Jewish cultural messages. Politicians and private institutions form a National Campaign to Prevent Jew Violence.

We need not add the seig-heils to realize that equating Jews and violence isn't an expression of science or genuine concern, but rank anti-Semitism. Linking an entire population class with a negative behavior practiced by only a few of its members is bigotry, regardless of which group is singled out. The politician-media-institution campaign on "youth violence" is bigoted and devoid of genuine concern for youths. Real concern would involve lamenting the major causes of violence against youths, yet politicians and institutions deploring "school violence" and pushing the National Campaign to Prevent Youth Violence concern themselves only with the tiny fraction of murdered children and youth that is politically advantageous to highlight while downplaying larger dangers to the young.

The target of aging America's rage is all youths, not just the 13 kids who committed the recently publicized shootings taking 31 lives in 12 schools in four years (in Pearl, Mississippi; West Paducah, Kentucky; Jonesboro, Arkansas; Edinboro, Pennsylvania; Springfield, Oregon; Littleton, Colorado; Conyers, Georgia; Fort Gibson, Oklahoma; Mount Morris, Michigan; West Palm Beach, Florida; Santee, California). These aren't all the school shooters; only the young ones with white victims we choose to care about. Compare: 25 million teenagers, 18 million of them white, attend 20,000 American secondary schools every day. Another 25 million pre-teens attend elementary schools.

Adults Commit More Gun Crimes

The FBI reports that youths under age 18 accounted for about 6% of the 50,000 murders in the U.S. [between 1996 and 2000.] The famous school shootings comprised one-twentieth of 1% of the murders in the United States, and half of these were at Littleton. By contrast, in a few months, over-30 men slaughtered three times more in multiple-victim shootings than all school students in four years [a Colorado high school].

Mike Males, *Kids and Guns: How Politicians, Experts, and the Press Fabricate Fear of Youth*, 2000.

"Columbine" (it seems a grievous injustice on top of tragedy to equate a school's name with mass murder) revealed the individual pathologies of two high school boys; "post-Columbine" revealed the mass pathology of America's institutions. In [2002], I still can't pick up a copy of *Youth Today* without seeing program ads blaring, "The Lessons of Columbine," crack a newspaper without seeing some Ph.D. declaiming "the new face of youth violence," glance at a magazine rack or turn a TV knob without confronting, "the secret life of suburban teens." The only blessing is that *Rolling Stone* fear-monger Randall Sullivan hasn't (yet) unburdened another of his fact-free histrionics anointing [Columbine shooters] Eric Harris and Dylan Klebold the new Everyteens.

The lesson of reporting on Columbine is pretty simple:

America sports an ugly new face of adult hostility, and it doesn't care about kids. It's the "quality," not the quantity, of school violence victims that sets off panic, with the paradoxical result that school murders actually are underreported. The late-1990s tactic by the media and officials to focus on demonizing suburban and small-town youth as the fright-provoking face of American savagery means that murders of poorer students and murders by adults in schools are systematically ignored. In a bizarre twist that reveals reams about official America's true concern for young people, whether kids are more likely to get hurt or killed in schools today than in the past, or more in danger in schools than elsewhere in society, is of little importance. The alarmism surrounds the supposedly new development that victims now are white —and thus politically useful.

Black and White

The National School Safety Center's [NSSC's] excellent tabulation of "School Associated Violent Deaths" (http://www.nsscl.org), covering the period from August 1992 through May 2003 (the latest as of this writing),[1] reveals how the press and politicians have relentlessly manipulated school violence. In truth, there were 39 additional school murders during 1999–2001 which received practically no publicity, resulting from 35 incidents involving 37 killers in cities from Hoboken, New Jersey, to Pomona, California. What made these 39 school murders worthy of silence? They fell into two categories. Thirty involved student victims who were black, Hispanic, Asian, or of unknown race (the eight whose races were not reported attended mostly-minority schools), killed by other students or by adults. Nine involved white victims: six were adults murdered by adults, two were students murdered by adults, and one student died from a previously undiscovered aneurysm after a fistfight. And if the NSSC's tabulation included preschools, the deliberate mowdown of two toddlers by an enraged middle-aged driver in Costa Mesa, California, would add to the school murder toll the media ignored.

In the super-charged 1999 school year when the media

1. Mike Males made some revisions to this viewpoint in 2004.

feverishly awaited any new school shooting, three were shrugged off. An Elgin, Illinois, 14-year-old was shot to death in his classroom in February. Not news: he was Latino and in special ed. On June 8, two girls were gunned down in front of their high school in Lynwood, California, south of Los Angeles. Not news (even to the *Los Angeles Times*, which ran a modest 440-word story on an inside page); they were Latinas. On November 19, a 13-year-old boy shot a 13-year-old girl to death in a Deming, New Mexico, middle school. Also Latinos, not the news editors' kind and therefore not news.

Similarly, the Santana High School shooting in Santee, California, on March 5, 2001, involving a white 15 year-old shooting to death two other white students alleged to have bullied him, received massive press attention. Reporters absurdly depicted Santee, site of considerable racial and domestic violence, as a pristine suburb menaced only by drug-taking teens. The school superintendent suspended friends of the student shooter, who were also badgered by the press for not reporting their vague suspicions; popular students suspected of bullying unpopular kids were not similarly taken to task. In addition, gun murders of two black and one Latino student in the two months surrounding Santee's killings were ignored. And, in a major irony that escaped much attention, a law enforcement officer training to respond to school shootings at a Texas high school accidentally shot a fellow officer to death on June 7, indicating that gunners who create danger at school are not all students.

In fact, several of the unheralded school murders (the multiple killings of white adults in Hoboken and Fort Lauderdale, Fla., in lover-triangle shootings, or of Latino students in Pomona and in Lynwood) had death tolls equaling or exceeding nationally headlined killings (Pearl and Springfield involved two killings, Edinboro and West Palm Beach one, Conyers and Fort Gibson none). Why, then, did the media, politicians, and quotable experts deem white-suburban-student murders an apocalypse and white-adult, minority-student, and inner-city killings of no importance?

To ask the question is to answer it: in the crass logic of reporters and editors, things like that are "supposed to happen" to darker skinned youth. The press's new mission was to demonstrate that school shootings proved white, suburban youth were out of control. If reporters had to ignore school killings that didn't confirm their narrow agenda, ignore them they did. . . .

Wrong Conclusions

The problem with deriving any "lessons" from Littleton is that the rare psychopath, by definition, does things for reasons the mass of non-psychopaths never consider. Nevertheless, books, documentaries, and "youth violence" treatises for years to come will feature highly credentialed authors selectively choosing whatever over-generalized "explanation" for the "why why why" suits their preconceived ideologies. I suggest we should pay more attention to Harris's quiet video aside: "I can make you believe anything." For this is all we really know about Klebold and Harris: along with Kip (Springfield) Kinkel, Michael (West Paducah) Carneal, and the handful of other school shooters, their kind is vanishingly rare among teenagers. Here is the irrefutable fact the school gunners proved: any youth can obtain hefty firepower within scant hours or days of wanting it, so if even one in 100,000 high schoolers harbored their murderous mentality, we'd have several Columbines and Jonesboros every week, not two or three a year. The most accurate conclusion is also the least satisfying to those bent on divining larger cultural "messages" from Columbine: Klebold and Harris represented Klebold and Harris, not a generation, not even alienated boys.

Now, what is preventing *Rolling Stone's* Randall Sullivan and other "experts" from pronouncing such an inescapable conclusion based on the evidence—the job of an expert, after all? In all the mass media freakout, I saw only one bit of sanity: CDC [Centers for Disease Control and Prevention] violence prevention epidemiologist Jim Mercy, who told *New York Times* reporter Sheryl Stolberg that school shootings are "the statistical equivalent of a needle in a haystack. The reality is that schools are very safe environments for kids."

The Real Culprits

Wait a minute, some might argue, when adults kill en masse, they get lots of bad press, too. Oklahoma City bomber Timothy McVeigh was deplored by the president and media for months. Daytrader Mark Barton, who gunned down 13 and wounded 25 at an Atlanta brokerage firm in August 1999, got on the covers of national magazines.

Are youthful killers being treated unfairly, then? No—youthful killers are not being mistreated, except in the sense that their evil deeds are more likely to be featured in the press and deplored by luminaries than similar murders by adults. (Dylan Klebold, Eric Harris, and Kip Kinkel remain far bigger names than Mark Barton, Buford Furrow, and Larry Gene Ashbrook, middle-agers who committed similar, more recent public massacres.) The unfairness involves the fact that middle-aged killers are treated by the press and experts as crazed individuals committing isolated acts while youthful killers are treated as part of a connected pattern demonstrating today's younger generation is uniquely barbaric. Consider recent murders in Ventura County, California, among the nation's richest suburban havens. Its three cities of over 100,000 people are regularly cited as among the safest in the United States from violent crime. Yet in . . . 36 months, three affluent, suburban Ventura grownups in their 40s blew away 10 people in multiple-victim rage shootings—six children and four adults. That's more than the combined toll of headlined shootings by high schoolers in Pearl, Mississippi; West Paducah, Kentucky; and Jonesboro, Arkansas—all in just one county.

Horror? The Ventura grownup shootings had that: 44-year-old man guns down screaming wife and three children on pastoral lane; 43-year-old man rakes two neighbors with bullets as one's three-year-old shrieks in terror; 42-year-old mom blasts three boys in their beds in ritzy rural enclave. All the usual big story ingredients were there: well-off perpetrators coldly mowing down innocent children in communities where "murder just doesn't happen," carnages so bloody law enforcement veterans required counseling, etc. Yet none made national headlines. No CNN continuous coverage, no Ph.D.s shaking heads at society's degeneration, no tearful presidential condolences. The only ingredient missing: the murderers were not youths.

The "post-Columbine" events proved the school shootings were not a youth, but a "dissed suburban male" phenomenon. The crucial point being missed is that Klebold, Harris, Kinkel, and other middle-class student gunmen had practically nothing in common with other kids (their isolation, in fact, was a big part of their rage), but they had a lot in common with adult middle-class mass killers. . . .

Myths and Overgeneralizations

"They're not drunk or high on drugs. They're not racists or Satanists or addicted to violent video games, movies, or music," began an April 9–10, 2000, *New York Times* series on school shooters and other "rampage killers," entitled, "They threaten, seethe, and unhinge, then kill in quantity." Reporters led by Ford Fessenden catalogued hundreds of rampage killings in the U.S. since 1950. They profiled 102 teenage and adult rampage murderers whose 100 multiple, public killings left 425 dead and 510 injured. As is nearly always the case when an issue is studied rather than butchered by experts' and pundits' anecdotal pontifications, the *Times* analysis uncovered major challenges to popular myths. Politicians' and programs' favorite culprits turned out to be trivial. Very few of the rampagers patronized violent media; practically none harbored occult or satanic interests. "Cultural *influences* seemed small," the *Times* concluded. However, there was "an extremely high association between violence and mental illness." Half had been formally diagnosed with serious maladies, led by schizophrenia and depression. When it came to ignoring warning signs of catastrophe, psychiatrists, family members, and peers were equally blind. Rampage killers overwhelmingly were male (96 of 102) and white (79). They tended to be older (high proportion in 30s and 40s) than single-victim murderers. A large majority were suburban, small-town, or rural.

Their mass killings were not new—not even school massacres. Two examples in the *Times* sample: in 1974, Olean, New York, honor student Anthony Barbaro, 17, opened fire at his school, killing three and wounding nine. In 1979, Brenda Spencer, 16, gunned two to death and injured nine at a San Diego elementary school. (Those two mass killings by white students in the 1970s merited only inside stories in

Time and *Newsweek*, which is why experts don't remember them.) But rampage killers of all ages, though rare, appear somewhat more plentiful today—23 per year in the 1970s and 1980s, 34 per year in the 1990s.

As noted, the FBI reports that youths under age 18 accounted for about 6% of the 50,000 murders in the U.S. in the last four years [prior to 2000]. The famous school shootings comprised one-twentieth of 1% of the murders in the United States, and half of these were at Littleton. By contrast, in a few months, over-30 men slaughtered three times more in multiple-victim shootings than all school students in four years. This raises a blunt question: do the authorities, from President Clinton to institutional and media commentators, view Cyrano Marks as a symbol of general murderousness among black men? Andrew Cunahan as a harbinger of gay male rage? Mark Barton as symbolic of suburban businessman savagery? Cora Caro as the image of the new killer soccer-mom? None I'm aware of has so labeled. In fact, most would consider those who define racial or other groups by their most brutal individuals as bigots of a particularly ugly and hostile mindset—especially if followed with proposals to inflict mass controls on the disfavored groups. It is exactly this kind of prejudicial thinking that grownups lecture teenagers to avoid.

Certainly there is no National Campaign to Prevent Middle-Aged Violence (which is a far more prevalent problem, statistically than "youth violence"). But if adults would not elevate our most murderous few as symbols of the moral disintegration of the groups we occupy, by what right do we hold up Klebold, Harris, or Kinkel as symbols of suburban youth, or of all youth?

*"In any given year, more than half of all
U.S. gun-related deaths are not homicides
at all, but suicides."*

Guns Contribute to High Suicide Rates

Chris Mooney

According to Chris Mooney in the following viewpoint, more than half of all gun-related deaths in the United States are suicides. Moreover, those who attempt suicide using a firearm are much more likely to succeed, Mooney contends. He also argues that people living in homes where guns are kept have a higher risk of suicide than those living in households without guns. Mooney is a Washington correspondent for *Seed* magazine and a senior correspondent for the *American Prospect*.

As you read, consider the following questions:

1. How many Americans kill themselves with a gun every day, as stated by Mooney?
2. According to the author, how many gun suicides and homicides were there in 1997?
3. According to Mooney, how has the NRA influenced the debate over gun-related suicides?

It was Sunday morning, Mother's Day. In Washington, D.C., the Clintons were welcoming Million Mom Marchers at the White House before their rally, while near the Washington Monument, the Second Amendment Sisters were beginning to assemble. But in North Michigan, in the town of Menominee near the Wisconsin border, it was also the morning after the local high school's prom, and B.J. Stupak, son of the four-term Democratic Congressman Bart Stupak, had been found dead in his home. The apparently thriving high school junior—recently elected president of the student council and named to prom court—had shot himself.

As Capitol Hill mourned the tragic death of Stupak's son, Republican Congresswoman Mary Bono decided something had to be done. She sent an open letter to the National Rifle Association's Wayne LaPierre, encouraging the group "to inform parents, teens and all gun owners of the potentially dangerous connection between the access to a gun and suicide." In B.J.'s case, the connection was lethal: According to police reports, the gun he used belonged to a family member.

There was painful irony to B.J. Stupak's death, in that his father is a member of the most visible organization promoting gun ownership; Stupak is one of Congress's few "NRA Democrats." A former police officer and state trooper, last year [1999] Bart Stupak said in an interview, "I'm a member of the NRA, my wife's a member of the NRA, our sons are members of the NRA."

Mary Bono's chief of staff Frank Cullen insists that "in no way was Congresswoman Bono attempting to characterize the incident" of B.J.'s death, or to speak for the Stupak family. Whatever the case, it was a rare, and slightly edgy moment: a Republican mother goading the NRA, while a Democratic father swallowed his grief.

The Crisis

Since the shootings at Columbine high school in April of 1999, stories of kids murdering kids have dominated gun control debates. But B.J. Stupak's death draws attention to an astonishing, but rarely cited figure: In any given year, more than half of all U.S. gun-related deaths are not homicides at all, but suicides.

According to some, this little known fact could help re-shape the gun issue. Today, the NRA insists that the only way for responsible Americans to protect their families from criminals is to own a gun—and countless families have acted on that warning. But what the organization fails to tell its members and others is that in most gun deaths, the shooter is also the victim.

Teen Suicide and Guns

As numerous studies have shown, guns are used in roughly two out of every three suicide attempts by teenagers, and handguns are used in 70% of these. In 1998 alone, 1200 youth in America committed suicide with a gun—the equivalent of one every seven hours.

"Teen Suicides and Guns," Handgun-Free America, 2005.

"If you really want to understand the issue of benefits and costs of firearms, you have to know what's happening with suicides," says David Hemenway, director of the Harvard Injury Control Research Center. What's happening is this: Suicide is the eighth leading cause of death in the U.S., and more Americans commit suicide using guns than with all other means combined. On average, 50 people kill themselves with guns every day.

In 1997, there were almost 18,000 gun suicides, compared to roughly 13,000 gun homicides. . . . In some states, the gun suicide to homicide ratio is actually far higher: In Colorado, for example, it is three to one.

Guns are also the most deadly weapon used in suicide attempts; guns kill more than nine out of 10 people who attempt suicide with them, according to one study. Since many suicide attempts are the result of impulsive behavior, this means access to a gun can easily turn a passing bout of depression into a tragedy. "If they didn't have [a gun] handy, they might try suicide by other means, but they'd be more likely to survive and get counseling," says Kristen Rand, federal affairs director at the Violence Policy Center.

But perhaps most significantly—and as Mary Bono's letter to the NRA pointed out—there appears to be a connection between gun availibility and risk of suicide, especially among youth. A number of studies, including several in the *New England Journal of Medicine*, have confirmed this link. According to the federal Centers for Disease Control and Prevention (CDC), "people living in households in which guns are kept have a risk of suicide that is five times greater than people living in households without guns."

Government's Silence

Despite these horrifying statistics, those in the federal government have only recently begun to talk about suicide—and they have almost completely ignored the gun connection. Indeed, although Senators Edward Kennedy, a Democrat from Massachusetts, and Pete Domenici, a Republican from New Mexico, have proposed legislation to devote $75 million for suicide prevention, their bill never mentions guns, instead focusing on mental health.

Last February [1999], a subcommittee of the Senate Appropriations Committee held the first congressional hearing on suicide prevention. Surgeon General David Satcher was a witness at the hearing; last year, Satcher declared suicide a serious public health threat and made it a top priority—becoming the first surgeon general ever to do so.

At the Senate's February suicide hearings, however, guns were barely mentioned. And indeed, the Surgeon General's groundbreaking suicide report has been taken to task by the Bell Campaign, a gun violence prevention group, for virtually ignoring gun suicide. "How does a major national health report overlook the cause of 17,700 deaths?" asks a release put out by the organization. The release adds, "Surely Surgeon General David Satcher understands the need to address guns as part of any meaningful plan to prevent suicide. But, like his predecessors, the Surgeon General must go to Congress for research funding. And, as we all know, Congress answers to the National Rifle Association."

The Campaign is right to implicate the NRA. Responding to those who charge that gun availability increases the chance of suicide, the NRA's Paul Blackman told *The Los Angeles Times*, "if a person is determined to kill himself, he will find a way." Not so, say some. As Emory University public health researcher Arthur Kellerman has written, "gun industry claims about the value of handguns for home defense are reminiscent of the early days of tobacco advertising, when cigarette companies extolled the health benefits of smoking."

In fact, the NRA is so determined to promote its viewpoint that it has found a way to quiet those who would publicize the facts that contradict it. (The organization did not return calls for this article.) The NRA successfully pressured Congress to cut funding for the Centers for Disease Control's effort to understand the public health effects of guns.

Gun control advocacy groups and suicide prevention organizations have been as uncoordinated as the NRA has been powerful. Some suicide prevention groups don't even take gun control positions, like the Colorado-based Yellow Ribbon Foundation. Though the American Foundation for Suicide Prevention and the American Association of Suicidology take strong stances, the latter's executive director, Dr. Alan Berman, nevertheless calls suicide "the invisible kid sister" in the gun debate.

Few Solutions

The result of this invisibility is that few have studied what kind of measures would specifically help reduce gun suicide. But some point to popular gun control proposals that could impact suicide levels—at least indirectly. Since many children and teenagers commit suicide with their parents' guns, experts say child trigger locks and smart gun technology (which would only allow a gun's owner to shoot it) would probably help prevent youth suicides. Likewise with President Clinton's proposed safe storage law holding parents responsible for making loaded, unlocked guns available to children. On the other hand, the elderly are a high-risk group for suicide—and a group for whom many such measures would be less effective.

A few suggest a more controversial approach: expanding background checks for gun purchases to include mental health records. After all, more than 90 percent of suicides are connected to some type of mental or substance abuse disorder. At present, federal law prohibits those who have been involuntarily committed to mental institutions from buying handguns. But law enforcement agencies do not have access to mental health records in most states, which means background checks frequently fail to prevent the mentally ill from buying guns. And that doesn't even begin to address those who have voluntarily entered mental institutions, or are simply receiving outpatient treatment. For these cases, many consider it crucial that at the very least, mental health professionals discuss the dangers of firearms with patients and their families.

Any discussion of using mental health records to prohibit people from buying guns raises a strong conflict, however. On the one hand, those concerned with suicide want to keep guns out of the hands of anyone who might consider it. On the other hand, some perceive such restrictions as unfair—and worry that expanding access to mental health records could violate patients' privacy.

The lack of proposals specifically designed to cut down on gun suicide only highlights the dearth of attention that the political and activist community has given the issue. Activists have treated suicide as a mental health issue only—excluding discussions of gun control to reduce suicide. And the NRA has ensured that the gun debate is centered on the criminal justice issue only—excluding discussions of gun control to reduce suicide.

But facts show that the debate must change. If stories like B.J. Stupak's begin to turn the debate toward the epidemic of gun suicide, perhaps the NRA will have to admit that a gun in the home is rarely a source of protection—and often leads to tragedy.

VIEWPOINT

6

"The weakness of the link between gun ownership and suicide should be obvious even to a two-year old."

Guns Do Not Contribute to High Suicide Rates

Nicki Fellenzer

Nicki Fellenzer argues in the following viewpoint that there is no connection between gun availability and suicide. Other factors such as social isolation and lack of mental health facilities cause suicides, she contends. Fellenzer also claims that suicide rates in developed nations with strict gun laws are actually higher than in the United States. Fellenzer is a contributing editor and writer for *Concealed Carry* magazine.

As you read, consider the following questions:
1. How many people killed themselves with a firearm in 2002, according to Fellenzer?
2. According to the Centers for Disease Control and Prevention, what is the crude suicide rate in the United States?
3. Of all the countries mentioned in this viewpoint, which one has the highest suicide rate?

Nicki Fellenzer, "The Politics of Suicide," *Armed Females of America*, 2005.
Copyright © 2005 by *Armed Females of America*. All rights reserved. Reproduced by permission.

The *New York Times* resident mouthpiece for the Brady Agenda [to ban guns] Fox Butterfield has filed a saccharine, angst-filled treatise on the "Culture of Suicide" [on February 13, 2005] in rural America. No doubt hanging for dear life on the coattails of the latest Brady wet dream—the death of a National Guard soldier in Maine and the subsequent battle of his mother to shred yet more of our rights— Butterfield has penned a clammy treatise blaming the availability of guns on high suicide rates in Stevensville, MT and other rural American areas.

You can almost see the tear streaks on Butterfield's quasi gut-wrenching discourse. Short, somber, single-sentence descriptive paragraphs open the curtain to the connective tissue between three melancholy lives—the gun that ended them. Continuing his tradition of promoting the gun banner agenda whenever possible, Butterfield has created a panorama of despair in rural America.

Individuality and self-reliance become a curse the could lead to suicide in the bizarre world Butterfield paints for Americans. "People who see themselves as rugged frontiersmen are often reluctant to reach out for help, particularly for mental health treatment," he writes. "If they do, they may see a physician instead of a psychiatrist or another trained mental health expert." And, of course, Fox wouldn't be Fox if he didn't throw in gun ownership as a "role" in suicide.

A Weak Link

The weakness of the link between gun ownership and suicide should be obvious even to a two-year old, but if Butterfield shows any understanding of the absurdity of his claims, it is overshadowed by his zeal to paint gun ownership as detrimental to mental health and stability.

"Researchers have long known the statistics, but new research illuminates the substantial role of firearms in suicide," he intones.

Well, OK. We'll give him that. According to the Centers for Disease Control, 31,655 people ended their lives in America in 2002. And more than half of those who chose to kill themselves—17,108—did so using a firearm.

But does this mean that gun ownership leads to greater suicide rates?

Does this mean that gun availability leads to an epidemic of self shootings?

Only if you believe that presence of toasters in the home leads to house fires. After all, nearly all the homes that burn down in America have a toaster! There *Must* be connection, right?

Suicide Demographics

It is true that suicide rates tend to be higher in rural areas. B. Dembling and L. Merkel, having studied suicide rates in rural Virginia conclude that, "Contrary to the traditional idea that rural areas are less stressed, more idyllic, and freer from violence and psychopathology than urban areas, recent research points to the fact that rural areas may have as much, if not more, violence and psychopathology than urban areas. This may be true of suicide as well. In addition, rural areas tend to have decreased access to resources and poorer health care delivery."

Residents in rural areas also tend to be poorer, according to the National Rural Health Association. On the average, per capita income is $7,417 lower than in urban areas, and rural Americans are more likely to live below the poverty level. The disparity in incomes is even greater for minorities living in rural areas. Nearly 24% of rural children live in poverty. This makes it a bit difficult to afford a shrink, when the cheapest of them charge $100 per hour.

There tends to be a sense of isolation in rural areas. Many times your closest neighbor is miles away. It's understandable that despite the idyllic, peaceful surroundings, depression could set in. It is also true that residents in rural areas tend to own firearms at a higher rate than their urban counterparts. Many large cities tightly control or ban firearms ownership, while Second Amendment freedoms thrive in America's rural lands. Hunting is a popular sport. Indeed, Butterfield confirms that in Stevensville, many students own firearms and hunt, often starting in junior high school. "Guns and hunting are a rite of passage in Montana," Linda Mullan, who works as a guidance counselor at Stevensville High school, said.

But what is completely incomprehensible is the insistence on *blaming* high rates of firearms ownership for high rates of suicide.

Social isolation is a direct cause of suicidal feelings. Lack of mental health facilities and the inability to afford psychiatric care can also be seen as a direct cause. But the easy availability of guns has no effect on the mental state of the owners or their ability to get help for those feelings of despair. The only thing firearms provide is a way for those who have already made the decision to end their lives to complete the act.

Gun Control and Suicide Rates

In the book *Point Blank: Guns and Violence in America*, Florida State University criminologist Gary Kleck analyzed suicide data for every American city with a population more than 100,000, and found no evidence that any form of gun control (including handgun prohibition) had an effect on the total suicide rate. Gun control did sometimes reduce gun suicide, but not overall suicide.

Notably, Japan, which prohibits handguns and rifles entirely, and regulates long guns very severely, has a suicide rate of more than twice the U.S. level. Many of the northern and central European nations also have very high suicide rates to accompany their strict guns laws. (Of course, if you have any suspicion that anybody in your home might be suicidal, it would hardly be a mistake for you to ensure that they do not have ready access to guns, tranquilizers, or other potentially lethal items.)

Dave Kopel, "The Fallacy of '43 to 1'," *National Review Online*, January 31, 2001. www.nationalreview.online.com.

Are they the only way? Of course not!

People who have reached a state of desperation so profound that they make the decision to quit, will not be deterred by the absence of a firearm. There are plenty of other ways one could end it all, including pills, household poisons and razors—all tools easily available and much more prevalent in America's households than firearms.

Suicide Rates in Other Countries

Additionally, if you compare suicide statistics from other nations—countries that either strictly regulate or restrict the ownership of firearms—you will see that the rural folks in the U.S. are relatively stable, even though their suicide rates tend to be higher than in urban areas.

According to the Centers for Disease Control, in the United States, the 2002 crude suicide rate per 100,000 among males was 17.95.

The World Health Organization, which keeps track of suicide rates in the world's nations, shows some numbers that could be alarming to Fox Butterfield and his band of hysterical cohorts at the *New York Times*, *if* they actually gave a damn about factual accuracy. In Australia, where the government continues to tighten its grip on gun owners and guns are becoming less and less readily available, 21.2 men per every 100,000 committed suicide in 1999.

In Austria—another gun control paradise—that number was 27.3.

In Belgium, in 1996, the suicide rate among men was 29.4 per 100,000

In Denmark—20.9 per 100,000 in 1998.

In Finland, where guns are strictly regulated, and you must have a damn good reason for owning one (apparently protection is not considered a valid need), 34.6 men per 100,000 offed themselves in 2000.

And in that socialist paradise, Japan, where the *only* reason you will ever be allowed to own a gun is if you participate in shooting sports, 36.5 men per 100,000 killed themselves in 1999.

Guns Are Not the Cause

What does this tell us?

It tells us that even though more than half of the people who commit suicide in the United States use firearms to do it, the high rate of firearms ownership is *not the cause* of the "Culture of Suicide" to which Butterfield alludes. Indeed, it appears that if people want to end it all, they'll do it using any means available, firearms or not. In rural America, guns appear to be the tool of choice. What do they use in Japan?

But then again, what do you expect from the *Times'* resident political activist for Handgun Control, Inc.—the truth? Some honest research? Please! Butterfield's hysterical gun control agenda-ridden dramatics were discredited by John Lott in *The Bias Against Guns*, and yet, he continues to spew melodramatic misrepresentations about guns and gun ownership in an obsequious effort to get just a quick lick of Sarah Brady's shoe.

But Fox need not look to rural Montana if he wants to wax sensational about suicides. He can stick closer to home. Apparently a rash of suicides at New York University about a year ago saw four students jump to their deaths from rooftops in a span of 6 months.

Using Butterfield's logic, may be tall buildings are to blame.

"Where the Bush administration's 'war on terror' has conflicted with the interests and raw political power of the gun lobby, mounting evidence shows that the war consistently loses."

Terrorists Procure Guns in America

Mark Benjamin

In the following viewpoint Mark Benjamin examines recently proposed legislation that would shield the gun industry from lawsuits, asserting that the bill will make it easier for individuals on the terrorist watch list to buy guns. He notes that gun shows remain a prime location for suspected terrorists to purchase firearms. Benjamin asserts that although most people think of terrorists using other types of weapons such as bombs, armed terrorists could kill hundreds of people at a time. The legislation passed in July 2005. Benjamin is a national correspondent for *Salon*.

As you read, consider the following questions:

1. According to a GAO report, how many individuals on the terrorist watch list have been able to buy guns?
2. What are two powerful weapons now legally available to terrorists, as described by Benjamin?
3. How will recently proposed legislation by Representative Larry Craig (R-ID) affect the problem of terrorists buying guns in the United States, according to the author?

When Idaho Republican Sen. Larry Craig introduced his bill last month [February 2005] to shield the gun industry from lawsuits, he claimed it was nearly identical to a similar measure that went down in a series of parliamentary maneuvers on the Senate floor in March 2004. The bill would quash all suits against the gun industry, except where evidence proves a dealer knowingly broke the law. When lawmakers come back from Easter recess, they're expected to take up the legislation, and with Congress more Republican and more pro-gun than it was last year, the bill is considered more likely to pass this time [it passed in July 2005].

But Craig has slipped in a so far widely unnoticed provision that gun industry experts say goes way beyond the one that died in the last Congress. It would bar "administrative proceedings" against the gun industry, which means that along with being immune from most lawsuits, dealers—even unscrupulous ones—would no longer have to worry about having their licenses revoked. The Bureau of Alcohol, Tobacco, Firearms and Explosives uses such administrative proceedings to regulate the gun industry. But under Craig's provision, the ATF's authority would be greatly curtailed.

When I showed the provision to some industry experts, they were stunned that Congress was poised to make gun dealers and manufacturers virtually free from the authority of both the courts and law enforcement. Robert Ricker, a gun control advocate and former gun industry lobbyist, said the new provision is a dream for the industry. "This is much broader than last year. The [National Rifle Association] has been able to sell this as protecting the Second Amendment. And it goes way beyond that."

The gun industry and its supporters defend the new bill, saying frivolous lawsuits threaten to bankrupt their companies and deal a blow to the economy as a whole—all for manufacturing a legal product that works as advertised. "To blame [the gun industry] for the criminal misuse of firearms that are lawfully manufactured and sold is unjust," Rodd Walton, general counsel of gun manufacturer SIGARMS Inc., told a congressional panel this month [March 2005].

But gun control advocates say they are dumbfounded by the timing of Congress' effort to indemnify the gun industry because it will come just weeks after the release of a troubling report on guns and terrorism. A Government Accountability Office [GAO] report released earlier this month [March 2005] said that at least 36 individuals on the federal terrorist "watch list" have walked into gun shops and bought weapons. The report makes the current effort in Congress to provide immunity to the industry painfully ironic to the gun control crowd. "It really ought to be an embarrassment that Congress would push this bill in the wake of a report that terrorists are buying guns over the counter," said Dennis Henigan, legal action project director at the Brady Center to Prevent Gun Violence.

Observers say the strange juxtaposition speaks to the momentous clout of the National Rifle Association and the gun industry—and may have exposed like never before a glaring blind spot in homeland security. Where the Bush administration's "war on terror" has conflicted with the interests and raw political power of the gun lobby, mounting evidence shows that the war consistently loses. Henigan noted that suspects on the government's terror watch list cannot board airplanes or cruise ships, but they can buy assault weapons. "There is no question that this radical pro-gun ideology trumps the war on terror," he said. "It is quite striking."

Some gun law experts say the Bush administration has shown a remarkable willingness to push the edge of the civil liberties envelope, citing the necessities of war—the "sneak and peak" provisions of the USA PATRIOT Act and the naming of U.S. citizens as "enemy combatants" being prime examples. But as conservatives have consolidated power since [the September 11, 2001, terrorist attacks], they have done little to stop would-be terrorists from arming themselves here in the United States. And as they have pursued an agenda that includes an ostensible dedication to preserving the sanctity of the Second Amendment, their success may have had the unintended consequence of making it easier, not harder, for terrorists to get guns.

"Nothing has been done, and in fact it has gone the other way," said Ricker. "Look at the whole way the administration has handled things since 9/11. There is a constitutional right to travel, for example, but [the administration is willing to] restrict rights to travel. They have [attacked terrorism] through banking and financial transactions. But as far as guns go—the Second Amendment—it is wide open."

Terrorists Are Legally Buying Guns

We rarely first think of terrorists' connections with guns so much as their use of other weapons, like explosives or hijacked airplanes. Yet, remember the indelible image of the crouching [September 11 terrorist-attacks mastermind] Osama Bin Laden, aiming an AK-47 assault weapon; or gun stockpiling [Oklahoma City bomber] Timothy McVeigh's obsession with *The Turner Diaries*, in which a gun enthusiast blows up FBI headquarters to protest tighter gun laws. Should armed terrorists attack a domestic target with assault weapons tomorrow, it would not be as if we weren't warned. The "How Can I Train Myself for Jihad" manual, reportedly found in safe houses in Kabul, Afghanistan, recommends that terrorists arm themselves with assault weapons. "In other countries, e.g. some states of USA, South Africa, it is perfectly legal for members of the public to own certain types of firearms," the manual says. "If you live in such a country, obtain an assault rifle legally, preferably AK-47 or variations, learn how to use it properly and go and practice in the areas allowed for such training." According to the GAO report, that is exactly what is happening.

In the January/February [2005] issue of the *Atlantic Monthly*, former national coordinator for security and counterterrorism Richard Clarke looks back on potential terror attack scenarios. In one, he imagined four terrorists attacking the Mall of America in Minnesota, armed with TEC-9 submachine guns, street-sweeper 12-gauge shotguns and dynamite. They killed 300 and wounded 400. "It had not been hard for the terrorists to buy all their guns, legally, in six different states across the Midwest," Clarke warns.

And indeed, as the GAO reported, it seems that some potential terrorists are buying guns legally. I wanted to see what they could get their hands on. After a 15-minute written safety quiz at the local National Rifle Association range in Northern Virginia (answers are provided), I put 34 bullets into the head and neck of a human-shaped target from 150 meters away, using an M-16 propped on a table and fitted with a small scope. I missed four times. I had never shot a gun before in my life, but I can go to the local gun shop and buy one. And a frightening array of weapons is now on the market that would put the M-16 to shame. Last November [2004], the Department of Homeland Security sent an "Officer Safety Alert" to agents warning them about the FN Herstal Five-Seven. It's a handgun that can penetrate body armor, a capability usually reserved for rifles. According to FN Herstal's Web site touting the gun: "Enemy personnel, even wearing body armor, can be effectively engaged up to 200 meters."

Tennessee-based Barrett Firearms Manufacturing makes the 82A1 .50 caliber sniper rifle. Accurate from a mile away, the rifle's huge round can go through an engine block or take down an airplane or helicopter. A May 2003 after-action report from an Army sniper team in Iraq with the 82nd Airborne describes the power of a Barrett .50 caliber sniper rifle. The report said the rifle was used "to engage both vehicular and personnel targets out to 1,400 meters." It said the snipers liked the rifle, in part, because of the "psychological impact on other combatants that viewed the destruction of the target." A sniper team using that rifle reported: "My spotter positively identified a target at 1,400 meters carrying [a rocket-propelled grenade] on a water tower. I engaged the target. The top half of the torso fell forward out of the tower and the lower portion remained in the tower." The report says that in some cases, targets were disintegrated when shot with the rifle. These guns are widely available, and no special license is needed to buy one.

No Accountability

If Craig's bill passes, the ATF will have little or no ability to take away the license of a dealer who unscrupulously allows Herstal Five-Sevens or .50 caliber sniper rifles to flow into the wrong hands. Joe Vince, the former chief of the ATF's Crime Gun Analysis Branch, said the bill's new provision barring "administrative proceedings" would severely hamper his old agency. "When they are talking about administrative, what that means is they cannot lose their license," Vince said. "So there is no regulatory power." The ATF reports that 1 percent of gun dealers are responsible for nearly 60 percent of the guns traced to a crime. Vince agreed that

Guns and Terror

As our nation conducts its war on terrorism—at home and abroad—one salient and unassailable fact is conspicuously absent from the national dialogue: terrorists and guns go together. The gun is part of the essential tool kit of domestic and foreign terrorists alike. Guns are used to commit terrorist acts, and guns are used by terrorists to resist law enforcement efforts at apprehension and arrest. The oft-seen file footage of Osama Bin Laden, aiming his AK-47 at an unknown target, is now a familiar reminder of the incontrovertible connection between terrorism and guns.

For terrorists around the world, the United States is the Great Gun Bazaar. The *Chicago Tribune* reported recently that, found among the mounds of rubble at a training facility in Kabul [Afghanistan] for a radical Pakistan-based Islamic terrorist organization, was a manual entitled "How Can I Train Myself for Jihad" containing an entire section on "Firearms Training." Tellingly, the manual singles out the United States for its easy availability of firearms and stipulates that al-Qaeda members living in the United States "obtain an assault weapon legally, preferably AK-47 or variations." Further, the manual sets forth guidelines for how would-be terrorists should conduct themselves in order to avoid arousing suspicion as they amass and transport firearms.

Despite the President's otherwise aggressive anti-terrorism program, the Bush Administration has a blind spot when it comes to guns. This is dramatically illustrated by the Administration's policy on the privacy of gun sale background check records. At a Senate hearing on December 6, [2001,] U.S. Attorney General John Ashcroft acknowledged that he had refused a request by the FBI—an agency within his own department—to use Brady Law criminal background check records to determine if any of 1,200 foreign nationals detained after the September 11 attacks had bought guns. Ashcroft cited "privacy" as the basis for denying the FBI's request. This concern for the "privacy" of background check records comes from the same Justice Department that is allowing government agents to monitor conversations between detainees and their attorneys.

Loren Berger and Dennis Hennigan, "Guns and Terror," The Brady Center to Prevent Gun Violence, 2001.

most gun dealers play by the rules. "So who are they protecting here?" Vince asked.

The sponsor of the House version of Craig's immunity

bill, Florida Republican Cliff Stearns, said the new language means the ATF can only take away a license if it can prove that a gun dealer "willfully or knowingly" violates the law—the same standard the bill sets up to let some lawsuits proceed. "If that's the case, the ATF can still revoke a license," Stearns said in a statement to *Salon*. A spokesman for Craig said the senator agrees with Stearns.

But Brian J. Siebel, a senior attorney at the Brady Center, disagrees. He said it is a "real admission" that Stearns admits he is curtailing the ATF's authority at all. He points out that the wording of the legislation does appear to tie the ATF's hands in all cases. "He is trying to pull the wool over your eyes," said Siebel.

Stearns and his supporters make a big deal out of the fact that their bill still holds dealers accountable to the ATF or the courts where it is clear a dealer purposely broke the law. But critics say gun dealers know the loopholes. In the case of the D.C. sniper, the bureau found that the dealer had lost 283 guns over three years, sparking allegations that it was actually illegally selling guns to criminals off the books. The gun dealer's inventory magically shrank while its guns showed up in the hands of criminals. There were no records proving the dealer knew he was breaking the law. That dealer, Bull's Eye, was among the top 1 percent of dealers in numbers of guns traced to a crime.

If Craig's legislation passes, it will be the latest in a long line of actions since Bush took office making powerful guns easier to get and harder to trace, even as politicians on both sides of the aisle claim to be getting tough on terrorism. In a speech to the United Nations soon after 9/11, Bush had called on the world to crack down on terrorists' financing, improve intelligence, coordinate law enforcement and keep guns out of terrorists' hands. "In this war on terror, each of us must answer for what we have done or what we have left undone," Bush told the U.N. General Assembly on Nov. 10, 2001. "We have a responsibility to deny weapons to terrorists and to actively prevent private citizens from providing them."

Yet, under a law Bush signed in January 2004, the government now destroys in 24 hours all records from background checks of gun purchasers. Critics had said keeping the records would help the government track fraud and abuse. In his hypothetical scenario at the Mall of America, Clarke writes: "This meant that if a gun buyer subsequently turned up on the new Integrated Watch List, or was discovered by law-enforcement officials to be a felon or a suspected terrorist, when government authorities tried to investigate the sale, the record of the purchase would already be on the way to the shredder." Right after 9/11, then–Attorney General John Ashcroft refused to give the FBI access to records that might have helped determine if any of the 1,200 people detained immediately after the attacks had sought to buy weapons.

In September 2004, Congress allowed the ban on assault weapons to expire. President Bush has said he supports the ban, and has faced harsh criticism for expending little political capital to extend it. Gun rights groups say the ban was mostly aesthetic. But perhaps most important, the ban also outlawed ammunition clips larger than 10 rounds. Now, clips are unregulated, giving potential terrorists more continuous firepower for their high-powered weapons.

Other Loopholes

While the government's "war on terror" continues, Congress also has not yet closed the "gun show loophole." Sales at gun shows are completely unregulated in most states, and most purchases require no background checks. There is concern that the shows are open-air bazaars for criminals, and possibly terrorists. Congress also passed what is known as the "Tiahrt Amendment," named after Kansas Republican Rep. Todd Tiahrt. It keeps secret from the public ATF data tracing weapons used in crimes.

Congress and the White House have also failed to close the loophole that allows people on federal watch lists to legally buy guns. Congress has previously come up with a raft of reasons to bar a gun purchase, such as the 1968 ban for felons or illegal immigrant status. But more than three years after 9/11, being a suspected terrorist doesn't disqualify one from buying a gun. FBI Director Robert Mueller told a House panel this month that perhaps that should be changed. "We ought to look at what can be done to perhaps modify the law to limit that person's access to a weapon," Mueller said.

Justice Department officials said no proposal to do that is forthcoming. Kevin Madden, a department spokesman, said preventing terrorists from buying guns might alert them that they were under surveillance. "The terrorist watch list is an intelligence watch list that is constantly evolving," Madden told me.

The ATF said it doesn't hunt terrorists, per se, but that it does go after gun criminals and hopes terrorists get caught in the net. "Our criminal efforts are also our terrorism efforts," said ATF spokesman Drew Wade. "We have to enforce the laws of the land. So hopefully enforcing the laws of the land will help with terrorism as well." The ATF said firearms investigations have increased 93 percent over the past five years, and the number of defendants referred for prosecution on firearms violations has increased 135 percent over the same period.

Ricker, the former gun show lobbyist, worries about indications that the new bill giving immunity to the gun industry will pass. He said he bets that few lawmakers even know about the provision that would hog-tie the ATF. "I think it is incredible that the Republicans are kowtowing to a strong political ally, . . . the NRA. That is now spilling over to things like this immunity bill. They just say, 'This is [about] guns; I'm voting for it.' They obviously have not even read the bill."

"For a terrorist to come to a gun show in America looking for weapons makes about as much sense as an American going to Peshawar looking for a bake sale."

Terrorists Do Not Procure Guns in America

Wayne LaPierre and James Jay Baker

Wayne LaPierre and James Jay Baker maintain in the following viewpoint that terrorists are not buying guns at American gun shows. They argue that terrorists have easy access to guns in their home countries and have no reason to purchase firearms in the United States. Moreover, according to LaPierre and Baker, tightening the laws governing gun show purchases would not stop terrorists from obtaining arms since purchasers would merely circumvent the laws. LaPierre is executive vice president and chief executive officer of the National Rifle Association (NRA). Baker is the former executive director of the Institute for Legislative Action for the NRA.

As you read, consider the following questions:

1. According to LaPierre and Baker, what is the true agenda of those concerned about terrorists buying guns in the United States?
2. What is the gun show law the authors refer to?
3. How many guns later used in criminal activity are purchased at gun shows, as cited by the authors?

From our earliest days, Americans have liked to meet at gun shows where grown children take grandfather's hunting rifle, and collectors can find rare and beautiful antique firearms. If you believe the gun-control lobby, this age-old American institution has somehow mutated into a bazaar for violent felons, gangs, drug dealers, and now, they claim, international terrorists.

In fact, AGS [Americans for Gun Safety] claims to have "uncovered" several cases in which they allege suspected terrorists used gun shows to avoid background checks in Michigan, Florida, and Texas. "We are deluding ourselves if we believe that terrorists operating in America are adverse to using guns," says Jonathan Cowan, the former Clinton-Cuomo aide who runs AGS. "In fact, an Internet Web site urging Jihad against this country tells terrorists to acquire guns in America." AGS adds, "Given all the evidence we have about terrorists arming themselves in America, we can't continue to have an honor system for terrorists at gun shows."

This would be alarming if it were true.

Exploiting America's Grief and Horror

Those who fret about the gun-show loophole strike the pose of reasonable people who just want to address a worrisome defect in national gun laws.

The truth is, AGS documents show that Mr. Cowan and company (assisted by a former Clinton political aide and a former gun advisor to Senator Chuck Schumer, the leader of the gun-ban corps in the Senate) are using AGS to advance their "top national priority . . . passage of licensing and/or registration in the next Congress."

In other words, they want every gun owner in America to be subject to harsh new laws that can only ultimately lead to confiscation. . . . "I grew up around gun shows," says the NRA's [National Rifle Association's] Chris Cox. "I don't ever recall seeing jet fuel, anthrax, or even boxcutters." Certainly, AGS's use of America's grief and horror in the wake of the September 11 attacks doesn't hold up.

AGS wants to inject "terrorism" into the firearm policy debate at any cost, and it is willing to employ serial lies to forge a link between "terrorist" cases and gun shows. AGS rests one of these cases not on the Middle East, but on Ireland. AGS continues to cite the case of an "IRA terrorist" even though the jury that convicted the man for firearm violations acquitted him of the specific charge that he was an IRA terrorist. It is also clear from the record that the guns in question were bought at gun shows by "straw" purchasers (people with "clean" records who are willing to violate federal law and illegally purchase firearms on behalf of criminals prohibited from doing so). Nothing in the legislation AGS is promoting would or could prevent people from breaking the law in this way.

And remember Ali Boumelhem . . . , who AGS says attended a Detroit-area gun show so he could ship guns to Lebanon? Convicted one day before the September 11 [2001] attacks of conspiring to smuggle guns and ammunition, he has become an AGS poster boy to spread the lie that gun shows are a steady source of guns for foreign terrorists. The truth is that after the FBI placed this convicted felon under surveillance, he was arrested, prosecuted, and convicted in federal court—proving that existing firearms laws can work. To suggest that he slipped through a "gun-show loophole" is misleading at best. Once again, the best evidence shows that this convicted felon worked through a straw purchaser. That's not a loophole. That's a crime. Again, nothing in the McCain "gun-show loophole" bill or any other proposal would prevent such an illegal act.

AGS also trotted out the case of a Texas man—but investigations failed to show he had any connection to any terrorist attacks. There is now no indication to believe that he ever shipped guns overseas or bought guns for any reason other than personal protection.

One thing is for sure. If terrorists come to America determined to find guns, they can do so, just like common street thugs. They may find some way to subvert the law and obtain their firearms from a gun show or a gun store. It is more likely that they will obtain their guns in the same manner criminals do every day, from other criminals.

Or they will bring them with them.

Throughout the heartland of terrorism in the Middle East, one can walk into many *souks* and find an astonishing array of firearms—machine guns, bazookas, and other weapons that are illegal or heavily restricted in the United States. For a terrorist to come to a gun show in America looking for weapons makes about as much sense as an American going to Peshawar looking for a bake sale.

Bogus Cases

Since [the September 11, 2001, terrorist attacks], a number of anti-gun organizations have attempted to paint gun show restrictions as connected to the war on terrorism. Mrs. Sarah Brady frantically warns, "Incredibly, our soldiers could be gunned down by foreign terrorists armed with firearms purchased at American gun shows." Fortunately, the situation is much less dire than the anti-gun groups warn. Indeed, two of the . . . "terrorist" cases they point to do not even have terrorists in them.

Last year [2001], four people, including Conor Claxton, were convicted of buying guns at Florida gun shows, and illegally smuggling them to Ireland. Prosecutors alleged that one of them, Conor Claxton, was buying the guns for the Irish Republican Army [a terrorist group]. Claxton *was* convicted of gun smuggling, but *not* of supplying guns to terrorists. The case counts as an incident of gun shows being used to supply terrorists only if one deliberately ignores the jury's findings of fact.

A second "gun show terrorist" case also may not have any terrorists in it. On October 30, 2001, federal prosecutors secured a guilty plea for immigration law violations by Muhammad Navid Asrar, an illegal alien from Pakistan. While illegally living in Texas, Asrar purchased several firearms at gun shows. In federal court, Asrar pleaded guilty to illegal possession of ammunition, since it is illegal for illegal aliens to possess firearms or ammunition. A federal grand jury is currently investigating whether Asrar has any ties with terrorists. So far, no one in the government has claimed that he does.

David Kopel and Alan Korwin, "Should Gun Shows Be Outlawed?" Second Amendment Project, January 23, 2002. www.davekopel.com.

Gun shows today are much more likely to attract undercover agents from the Bureau of Alcohol, Tobacco and Firearms [BATF], the FBI, and the state police than Middle Eastern terrorists. There simply is no national security case to be made to crack down on this beloved American institution.

There Is *No* Gun-Show Loophole

The gun controllers conveniently forget to mention the most important aspect of each of their examples. In every case, the system worked. The violators were arrested, tried, and convicted. What does the law say now? *Convicted felons face a possible ten-year prison sentence just for touching a gun at a gun show. Federal law already prohibits nonresident and illegal aliens from buying guns.* Unlike the infamous cash-and-carry arms bazaars of the Middle East, licensed dealers at U.S. gun shows must perform the same background checks and fill out the same federal forms as they do when selling a gun in a store. Anyone who is in the business of selling firearms must obtain a Federal Firearms License from the BATF. That's the law already.

Fiction: Gun-control groups claim that 50 percent to 75 percent of guns used in crimes come from gun shows.

Fact: A 1997 National Institute of Justice study reported that only 2 percent of criminal guns came from gun shows. Another report in that year by the U.S. Bureau of Justice Statistics on federal firearms offenders reported that only 1.7 percent of guns used in crime were acquired at a gun show. Numerous other studies came to these same, fractional results—and in many of these cases, the criminals used straw purchasers. The fact is, gun shows are open, friendly, and public. They provide the kind of well-lit attention criminals do not like.

Still, there must be something that the gun controllers can hang their hats on, right?

Here it is. In the 1990s, a National Instant Check System (NICS) went into effect, a computerized database of people with criminal records who are disqualified from acquiring firearms. Under instant check, dealers must clear every firearms purchase through a background check with the FBI. Each dealer is given a Federal Firearms License number, a unique password, and information on the prospective buyer —name, date of birth, sex, and race (why the federal government should record that is anyone's guess), as well as the type of gun sought.

An operator checks the data against the instant check database. If you are not a prohibited person, you get your gun. If the check turns up ambiguous information (maybe someone else with your name in your state who has a criminal record), an analyst looks over the data. By law, the analyst has to approve or deny the sale within three business days, or the purchase may proceed.

The majority of gun-show sellers are licensed dealers. By law, they must conduct these checks.

However, this requirement for federal licensing and the background check does not extend to people who occasionally sell or trade guns from their personal collections. This is not a loophole. This is an acknowledgment that people like to trade and sell guns, just as they like to hold garage sales. Congress made sure that the widow selling her husband's hunting rifle or the collector ogling that Winchester rifle with the stock of Swedish pine would not have to bear the fees, wait, and paperwork burden of filling out Federal Firearm Licenses with the BATF if they get together on their own to make a deal.

Congress wisely recognized that people will do this. Hunters sell guns from their homes, through classified ads, and at their clubs and ranges. A gun show is just a place for them to meet. Outlaw these transactions in ordinary, everyday commerce, and you won't be doing anything to make life harder for criminals. Remember, gun commerce by violent criminals, drug dealers, fugitives, and illegal aliens is already a crime. Simple gun possession by a prohibited person is already a federal felony punishable by ten years in the federal slammer.

By putting all private sales under the heavy hand of the government, the gun-control lobby seeks to criminalize millions of law-abiding Americans. That, of course, is their intent: to criminalize so they can control.

Periodical Bibliography

The following articles have been selected to supplement the diverse views presented in this chapter.

John Buell — "Alternative Perspectives on School Violence," *Humanist*, September 2001.

Philip Cohen — "American Tales of Guns and Ignorance," *New Scientist*, December 25, 2004.

Nicolas Confessore — "Control Freaks," *American Prospect*, April 8, 2002.

Bill Durston — "Terminate This Epidemic," *Sacramento News & Reviews*, August 5, 2004.

Abigail Kohn — "Their Aim Is True," *Reason*, May 2001.

Dave Kopel — "America's Fascination with Firearms," *World & I*, October 2003.

Dave Kopel — "Two Cheers for Violence," *Liberty*, September 2004.

Jackson Lears — "The Shooting Game," *New Republic*, January 22, 2001.

John J. Miller — "High Caliber Advocacy: How the NRA Won the Fight over Gun Rights," *National Review*, February 13, 2005.

Steven Riczo — "Guns, America, and the 21st Century," *USA Today Magazine*, March 2001.

Sarah A. Webster — "Range of Injuries Shatters Stereotypes," *Detroit News*, November 27, 2000.

Franklin E. Zimring — "Firearms, Violence, and the Potential Impact of Firearms Control," *Journal of Law, Medicine & Ethics*, Spring 2004.

CHAPTER 2

Does Private Gun Ownership Reduce the Threat of Gun Violence?

Chapter Preface

In September 2004 Congress and the Bush administration let the contentious assault weapons ban expire, reigniting the debate over these firearms. Critics of assault weapons—semiautomatic guns that fire numerous rounds in a short period of time—contend that they have no legitimate purpose and should be banned. Other experts maintain that any ban on assault weapons would be unconstitutional.

Gun control advocates and law enforcement organizations across the country point out that assault weapons are designed to kill large numbers of people quickly, which makes them weapons of choice for gang members, drug dealers, and school shooters. They also argue that assault weapons pose a serious threat to law enforcement. In a 1993 report entitled *Officer Down: Assault Weapons and the War on Law Enforcement*, analysts at the Violence Policy Center claim that one in five law enforcement officers slain in the line of duty between 1998 and 2001 were killed with assault weapons. They cite the example of the murder of officers Charles Ezernack and Jeremy Carruth on February 20, 2003, in Alexandria, Louisiana. These two officers were killed in an ambush by Anthony Molette, who was using an AK-47 assault rifle. National law enforcement organizations, associations, and unions feel so strongly about the importance of the ban that they called for its renewal in 2004.

On the other side of the issue, gun rights advocates argue that owning assault weapons is protected under the Second Amendment, and that therefore the ban was a violation of an individual's right to bear arms. Lobbying organizations like the National Rifle Association viewed the ban as another step on the slippery slope to the revocation of all gun rights. They also argued that the ban did not make Americans any safer. Opponents of the assault weapons ban not only deride its effectiveness but also claim that assault weapons are not a major threat to law enforcement personnel. They argue that assault weapons are not the weapons of choice among drug dealers, gang members, or criminals in general. They note that these weapons are used in only about one-fifth of 1 percent of all violent crimes and in approximately 1 percent of all gun crimes.

In fact, assault weapons are not a common weapon: There are close to 4 million assault weapons in the United States, which is about 1.7 percent of the total gun stock.

With the sunset of the assault weapons ban in 2004, the debate over these firearms has intensified. Gun control advocates continue to press for a stronger, permanent ban on assault weapons while gun rights proponents argue that such a ban would be unconstitutional and ineffective. Like other aspects of the debate over gun ownership discussed in this chapter, the controversy over the assault weapons ban will likely continue well into the future.

"*It's a myth that the high gun ownership rate is a cause of the high murder rate in the United States.*"

Gun Ownership Deters Violent Crime

Robert A. Levy

In the following viewpoint Robert A. Levy presents statistics suggesting that gun ownership protects individuals from violent crime. He notes that self-defensive gun use is much more prevalent than gun-related crimes in any given year. Levy is a senior fellow in constitutional studies at the Cato Institute, a libertarian public policy research foundation. He is also a director of the Institute for Justice, a libertarian law firm, and a member of the board of visitors of the Federalist Society, a conservative and libertarian law policy group.

As you read, consider the following questions:

1. As stated by Levy, how many criminals are killed every year by civilians with guns?
2. Which state has the country's most permissive gun laws, according to Levy?
3. After Australia was disarmed in 1988, what happened to the country's violent crime rate, as related by the author?

Although Congress and the majority of state legislatures have resisted enacting draconian gun control laws, the courts are the final bulwark in safeguarding our constitutional right to keep and bear arms. Yet the courts of late have been the scene of unprecedented attacks on that right as gun control advocates have used the judiciary to make an end-run around the legislative process. Meritless litigation brought by government plaintiffs in multiple jurisdictions are just part of a scheme to force gun makers to adopt policies that legislatures have wisely rejected. Moreover, the suits are used by politicians to reward their allies—private attorneys, many of whom are major campaign contributors—with lucrative contingency fee contracts.

Meanwhile, many of the same politicians have exploited a few recent tragedies to promote their anti-gun agenda. But gun controls haven't worked and more controls won't help. In fact, many of the recommended regulations will make matters worse by stripping law-abiding citizens of their most effective means of self-defense. Violence in America is due not to the availability of guns but to social pathologies—illegitimacy, dysfunctional schools, and drug and alcohol abuse. Historically, more gun laws have gone hand in hand with an explosion of violent crime. Only during the past decade—with vigorous law enforcement, a booming economy, and an older population—have we seen dramatic reductions in violence, coupled with a record number of guns in circulation.

Before we compromise constitutional rights expressly recognized in the Second Amendment, we ought to be sure of three things: first, that we've identified the real problem; second, that we've pinpointed its cause; and, third, that our remedy is no more extensive than necessary to fix the problem. The spreading litigation against gun makers fails all three tests as do the latest gun control proposals. Guns do not increase violence; they reduce violence. Banning or regulating firearms will not eliminate the underlying pathologies. And a less invasive remedy already exists: enforce existing laws. . . .

Guns, Crime, and Accidents

Paradoxically, politicians who are busily abusing the rule of law and zealots eager to put gun makers out of business overlook compelling statistics suggesting that the anti-gun crusade, if successful, would leave Americans more, not less, susceptible to gun violence. Three thousand criminals are lawfully killed each year by armed civilians. By comparison, fewer than 1,000 criminals are killed annually by police. Guns are used defensively—often merely brandished, not fired—more than 2 million times per year. That's far more than the 483,000 gun-related crimes reported to police in 1996.

Our country's most permissive "gun-carry laws" are in Vermont, which has a very low crime rate. Nationwide, as Yale scholar John Lott has demonstrated, the larger the number of "carry permits" in a state, the larger the drop in violent crime. Half of our population lives in 31 states that have "shall issue" laws, which mandate that a permit be granted to anyone above the age of 21 who is mentally competent, has no criminal record, pays the requisite fee, and passes a gun safety course. Those states haven't turned into Dodge City, writes columnist Jonathan Rauch [in *National Review*, March 19, 1999], "with fender-benders becoming hailstorms of lead."

Actually, data show that Dodge City was safer than today's Washington, D.C., which has the highest gun murder rate in the United States, accompanied by the strictest gun control. Is that because guns are readily available in nearby Virginia? Then why is the D.C. murder rate 57 per 100,000 while Arlington, Virginia, an urban community just across the river, has a rate of 1.6 per 100,000? The answer is that social pathologies in D.C. promote crime, whereas guns in Virginia deter crime.

The reality is that less than 5 percent of the population take out concealed handgun permits. The rest of us benefit because the criminals don't know which 5 percent are armed. Laws permitting the carrying of concealed handguns reduce murder by about 8 percent and rape by about 5 percent. Police carry guns; mayors and bodyguards carry guns; why not law abiding residents of high-crime areas?

In May 2000 the House of Representatives passed (by voice vote with almost no debate) a bill permitting federal judges (including bankruptcy judges and even some retired judges) to carry concealed guns in any state, despite state laws to the contrary. A Florida federal district judge, Harvey

Schlesinger [in *CQ Weekly*, May 27, 2000] had this to say: "If a judge is in danger, the fact that he or she is in one state or the other does not eliminate the danger." He might have made the same statement about any person at risk.

Gun Crime in Other Countries

It's a myth that the high gun ownership rate is a cause of the high murder rate in the United States. In Australia, for example, the population was disarmed in 1998. Since then, homicides are up 3.2 percent, assaults up 8.6 percent, and armed robberies up 44 percent. In the preceding 25 years, armed robberies and homicides committed with firearms had declined. The Swiss, Finns, and New Zealanders each have an ownership rate similar to ours, but we have a far higher murder rate. In Israel, gun ownership is 40 percent above the U.S. rate, but the murder rate is far lower. When all countries are studied, there is no correlation between gun ownership and murder rates.

Interestingly, in Israel armed teachers are common and the threat of terrorism is pervasive, yet there are few terrorist attacks at schools. That's because armed civilians deter crime. An armed gun store employee in Santa Clara, California, shot a customer who had threatened to kill three others. Armed citizens prevented massacres in Anniston, Alabama; Pearl, Mississippi; and Edinboro, Pennsylvania. Yet the response of some politicians to such incidents is to disarm those very same citizens. Meanwhile, madmen in Rwanda murdered almost a million people in less than four months using nothing but machetes.

Guns in the Home

Advocates of gun control reject that analysis and point instead to a study by Arthur Kellerman, who concluded that families possessing a gun are 22 times more likely to kill a family member or acquaintance than to kill in self-defense. But what is not factored into the Kellerman equation is that guns are rarely fired; the value of the gun is to deter, not to kill. Moreover, 85 percent of the deaths that Kellerman cites are suicides. He explains that suicides are five times more likely if there is a gun in the home. But that assumes a particular causal relationship. It is just as likely that suicidal people acquire a gun precisely because they intend, or may be psychologically prone, to commit suicide.

Behaviors of Gun Carriers

Carried Gun for		
Target Practice	70.1%	
Hunting	46.7	
Protection	41.6	
Work	10.7	

Gun Carried in Car	51.6%	

	In General	When in Car
Usually Gun Was Loaded	40.0%	45.3%

How Carried Gun		
Visibly	23.9%	
Concealed on Person	23.1	
In Bag/Briefcase	33.3	
Other	14.1	
Don't Know	2.0	
Missing	3.5	

Ever Displayed Gun in Response to Threat	2.8%	

Gun Carrying Makes Person Feel		
Safer	59.4%	
Same	26.5	
Less Safe	9.8	
Don't Know/Missing	4.3	

Tom W. Smith, "Gun Carrying Behaviors of Gun Carriers," *2001 National Gun Policy Survey of the National Opinion Research Center: Research Findings*, National Opinion Research Center, 2001.

Again conflating cause and effect, Kellerman notes that a handgun in the home raises the risk of death by 3.4 times. Yet he overlooks the strong possibility that people at risk buy guns; the risk motivates the purchase, not vice versa. By analogy, a storeowner might decide to put iron bars on his store windows if the store were located in a high crime area. Surely, no one would suggest that the store would be safer if it removed the bars. Nor would a family in a high-risk inner-city environment be safer if it got rid of its handgun. The gun, like the bars, serves to safeguard lives and property. Remember that each individual could well be the sole means of his own defense. In the words of [David B.] Kopel and [Richard] Gardiner:

> Governments are immune from suit for failure—even grossly negligent or deliberate failure—to protect citizens from crime. Similarly, governments are immune from suit for injuries inflicted by criminals who were given early release on parole. Accordingly, it would be highly inappropriate for the government, through the courts, to make it . . . impossible for persons to own handguns for self-defense because, supposedly, ordinary Americans are too stupid and clumsy to use them effectively. If the Judiciary will not question the government's civil immunity for failure to protect people, the courts certainly should not let themselves become a vehicle that deprives people of the tools they need to protect themselves. Ask yourself whether you'd be willing to put a sign on your house stating, "This home is a gun-free zone"—especially if you lived in the inner city.

Guns and African Americans

While we're on the topic of the inner city, the head of the National Association for the Advancement of Colored People, Kweisi Mfume, acknowledges that there are "pathologies in any society that contribute to violence"—for example, teenage pregnancy, dysfunctional schools, drug and alcohol abuse, and a welfare system that subsidizes illegitimacy and unemployment. And [Robert J.] Cottrol reminds us that in the late 19th and early 20th century state gun control laws were aimed specifically at keeping guns away from former slaves, other blacks, and recent immigrants. Cottrol, a self-described Hubert Humphrey Democrat, also writes that "bans on firearms ownership in public housing, the constant effort to ban pistols poor people can afford—scornfully labeled 'Saturday Night Specials' and more recently 'junk guns'—are denying the means of self-defense to entire communities in a failed attempt to disarm criminal predators."

Or listen to Gregory Kane, an African-American columnist for the *Baltimore Sun*: "The NAACP should be assuring that every law-abiding citizen in America's black communities has a safe, affordable handgun. . . . These young men are smart enough to know that the combined forces of city and

91

state governments, Bill Clinton, the police, the NAACP, and the outrage of gun controllers won't protect them." Civil rights activist Charles Evers was even more blunt: "I put my trust in God and my .45 . . . and not always in that order."

One would have thought that, before filing its lawsuit, the NAACP would have examined the historical record. In 1967, a 13-year-old could buy a rifle from most hardware stores or even through the mail. Very few states had retail age restrictions for handguns. Until 1969, most New York City high schools had a shooting club; students regularly competed in shooting contests; and the federal government paid for rifles and ammunition. Federal and state gun laws today are far more restrictive than they were three decades ago. Yet, until the 1990s, more laws went hand in hand with an explosion of violent crime.

When gun ownership rates were constant through the 1960s and 1970s, violent crime skyrocketed. With ownership rates growing during the 1990s, we have seen dramatic reductions in crime. Recent statistics from the U.S. Bureau of Justice show that gun deaths and woundings declined by 33 percent from 1993 through 1997, with the decline continuing in 1998. Over the same interval, the number of guns in the United States grew by 10 percent. In short, despite misleading reports from the media, there is no evidence to suggest that gun ownership and violent crime are directly linked.

"There is . . . little credible evidence that guns deter crime."

Gun Ownership Does Not Deter Violent Crime

David Hemenway

In the following viewpoint David Hemenway asserts that contrary to the claims of the gun lobby, there is little credible evidence that guns deter violent crime. He cites studies that provide evidence that where there are more guns, there are more gun robberies and robbery homicides. Hemenway is a professor of health policy at the Harvard School of Public Health and director of Harvard's Injury Control Research Center and Youth Violence Prevention Center.

As you read, consider the following questions:

1. When the town of Morton Grove, Illinois, banned handguns, what was the effect on burglary rates, according to Hemenway?
2. What do credible studies find concerning cities, states, and regions where there are more guns, as cited by the author?
3. What did the Uniform Crime Reports and the U.S. National Crime Victimization Survey conclude about the relationship between gun ownership and crime?

Given the claims of the gun lobby, it is perhaps surprising that there is in fact little credible evidence that guns deter crime. Criminologist Gary Kleck claims that publicized police programs to train citizens in gun use in Orlando (to prevent rape) and in Kansas City (to prevent robbery) led to reductions in crime by changing prospective criminals' awareness of gun ownership among potential victims. However, a careful analysis of the data found no evidence that crime rates changed in either location after the training. The deterrent effects of civilian gun ownership on burglary rates were also supposedly shown by the experiences of Morton Grove, Illinois (after it banned handguns), and Kennesaw, Georgia (after it required that firearms be kept in all homes). Again, a careful analysis of the data did not show that guns reduced crime. Instead, in Morton Grove, the banning of handguns was followed by a large and statistically significant decrease in burglary reports.

Suspect Studies

The fact that rural areas in the United States have more guns and less crime than urban areas has sometimes been claimed as evidence of the deterrent that firearms represent. The comparison, of course, is inappropriate. Cities in high-income countries generally experience more crime than rural areas, whatever the levels of gun ownership. A more valid comparison is between cities, between states, or between regions.

One study found a negative association between rates of gun ownership and crime rates (more guns, less crime). However, in that study, gun ownership data came from election exit polls conducted in 1988 and 1996. These data on gun ownership levels are unreliable. According to the polling source, Voter News Service, the data cannot be used as the author uses them—to determine either state-level gun ownership levels or changes in gun ownership rates—for three reasons: (1) the survey sampled only actual voters, a minority of the adult population; (2) the gun ownership question changed between the two periods; and (3) the sample size was far too small for reliable estimates. In only fourteen states were there more than one hundred respondents to the 1996 poll, and for one such state, Illinois, the polls indicated, nonsensically, that personal gun ownership more than doubled between 1988 and 1996, from 17 to 36 percent of the adult population. Overall, the data from these exit polls indicate that gun ownership rates in the United States increased an incredible 50 percent during those eight years. Yet all other surveys of the general population show either no change or a decrease in the percentage of Americans who personally own firearms. Analyses of guns and crime using the Voter News Service data are meaningless.

No other study finds that crime is lower in cities, states, or regions where there are more guns. Instead, the evidence indicates that where there are more guns, while there are no more robberies, there are more gun robberies and more robbery homicides. Most studies find that where there are more guns, there are significantly more gun homicides and total homicides.

A widely cited proponent of the supposed deterrent effect of guns has claimed that when gun prevalence is high, burglars seek out unoccupied dwellings to avoid being shot. Yet the evidence comes not from a scientific study but from a flawed comparison using different victimization surveys in different time periods for four areas—the United States, Britain, the Netherlands, and Toronto. In the United States, compared to the other three areas, a higher percentage of burglaries are committed when no one is at home. [Gary] Kleck's analysis does not take into account relevant factors that might explain the association (e.g., the percentage of time in which dwellings are occupied). The areas are compared to the United States but not to each other, and only four nations/cities are examined. One could just as well argue that since cigarette consumption is higher in Japan and Stockholm than in the United States, and the Japanese and Swedish live longer than Americans, cigarettes are good for longevity.

A more reliable study used data from the Uniform Crime Reports for all fifty U.S. states for 1977–98 and data from the U.S. National Crime Victimization Survey (NCVS) for 330,000 households for 1994–98. The findings from both analyses were that U.S. counties and states with more guns have higher rates of burglary and higher per capita rates of "hot burglary" (burglary when someone is at home). Homes with firearm collections are considered prime targets for burglars.

Who Owns Guns?

1. Both household and personal ownership is greater among men than women.

2. Ownership is lowest in large cities and greatest in rural areas. Likewise it is lowest in the more urban Northeast and higher in more rural regions.

3. The married are most likely to have guns in general, with the never married and separated the least likely to have a weapon.

4. Gun ownership varies little by educational level.

5. Gun ownership increases with household income, but for household presence it appears to fall-off among those with incomes over $80,000.

6. Gun ownership is highest for the middle aged. Adults under 30 and over 65 are less likely have a gun in their household. However, personal ownership of a gun does not fall-off among older adults. The lower levels among younger adults is partly due to the decline in hunting over the last 25 years.

7. Households with two children are the most likely to have a gun in general or a handgun in particular (but the difference for handguns is not statistically significant). Personal ownership varies significantly, but irregularly, by number of children.

8. All forms of gun ownership are greater among conservatives, lowest among liberals, and intermediate for moderates.

9. Whites show higher ownership levels than Blacks, but none of the differences are statistically significant.

Tom W. Smith, *2001 National Gun Policy Survey of the National Opinion Research Center: Research Findings*, National Opinion Research Center, 2001.

Surveys of burglars in the United States do indicate that most would prefer that no one is at home—and presumably that no one is armed—when they enter the premises. There is little question that professional burglars, who are among the least violent of serious criminals, want merchandise and do not want to get arrested, bludgeoned, or shot. But there is currently no credible evidence that a high prevalence of gun ownership reduces burglary or any other crime or in any way reduces potential violent confrontations. . . .

Self-Defense and Gun Use

Self-defense gun use is a somewhat nebulous concept. Criminals, for example, often claim that they carry guns for protection and use them during crimes in self-defense because they felt threatened by the victim. Most of the self-defense gun uses reported on private surveys appear to be both illegal and against the public's health and welfare. Of course, there are undoubtedly many instances of successful and socially beneficial self-defense gun uses. Each month, the *American Rifleman*, the magazine of the National Rifle Association, features about a dozen accounts of armed citizens defending themselves based on newspaper clippings submitted by NRA members. Yet even these stories may not always be what they purport to be.

Surprisingly, although protection and self-defense are the main justifications for a heavily armed citizenry, there is little evidence of any net public health benefit from guns. No credible evidence exists for a general deterrent effect of firearms. Gun use in self-defense is rare, and it appears that using a gun in self-defense is no more likely to reduce the chance of being injured during a crime than various other forms of protective action. No evidence seems to exist that gun use in self-defense reduces the risk of death; case-control studies of firearms in the home fail to find any life-saving benefit, even when exclusively considering cases involving forced entry.

Whatever one thinks about the benefits of self-defense gun use, reasonable gun policies—such as requiring manufacturers to meet minimum safety standards or requiring background checks on sales at gun show—would have little effect on the ability of responsible adults in the United States to defend themselves with guns.

*"As a police officer, I would actually feel
safer knowing we had trained civilians
who could help me when I needed it."*

Concealed Weapons Make Society Safer

Steve Newton

In the following viewpoint Steve Newton claims that an
armed populace can fight violent crimes and terrorism. He
contends that allowing citizens to carry concealed weapons
will make police officers safer as well; armed citizens could
help police when needed, he argues. He also claims that
more officers are killed by accidents than by criminals' guns.
Newton is the vice president of the National Association of
Chiefs of Police.

As you read, consider the following questions:
1. In 1999, how many police officers were killed in the line
   of duty with a firearm, as stated by Newton?
2. According to the author, how do concealed weapons
   laws help in the war on terror?
3. According to the NRA, how many defensive gun uses
   are there every year?

B eing an old police chief, I have had the opportunity to meet many politicians and almost invariably they will question me regarding my opinion on the right of citizens to carry concealed weapons. When I state my position that I think it's a good idea, we usually wind up in a heated discussion about the evils of guns and all the harm they do. I remember a Governor telling me that he could not believe any police chief would be for carrying weapons when so many police officers die every year from being shot.

The Toll on Police Officers

Well, what do you say to something like that? Most of the time you are not going to change any minds but I do wish they would at least get the facts straight. Number one, no one knows better than I do how many fine people we lose every year. Being the Vice President of the National Association of Chiefs of Police, I see the thousands of names on our memorial wall and I grieve for every one. However, I believe that most officers killed with a firearm are killed by criminals and not law-abiding citizens. I also believe that the argument to outlaw firearms or deny the right to carry because of the danger to police officers is a false one. Let's look at some statistics:

In 1999, nationally, 42 law enforcement officers were feloniously killed in the line of duty. 23 slain officers were municipal, 13 were county, 5 were state and 1 federal officer. Firearms were used in 41 of the 42 deaths. 25 were handguns, 11 were rifles and 5 were shotguns. 5 officers were slain with their own service weapons. 20 officers were murdered in the South, 11 in the West, 6 in the Midwest and 5 in the Northeast.

12 officers were killed during arrest situations, 6 were serving arrest warrants, 4 were trying to prevent robberies or apprehend robbery suspects and 2 were investigating drug situations. Also 8 officers were slain while enforcing traffic laws, 7 while investigating suspicious persons, 7 while answering disturbance calls, 6 in ambush situations and 2 while handling prisoners.

Now here is food for thought. An additional 65 officers were *Accidentally Killed* in 1999 while performing their duties. 51 were killed in car, motorcycle or aircraft accidents. 9 officers were accidentally struck by vehicles, 3 were accidentally shot, 1 was killed in a fall and 1 was killed in an all terrain vehicle accident. In other words, in 1999, more law enforcement officers were killed by accident than by firearms. Not only that, but of the 55,026 line of duty assaults on officers, 81.5 percent were committed with personal weapons. (Hands, feet, fist, etc.) Statistics provided by the FBI, released March 15th, 2001.

Tinsley. © 1996 by King Features Syndicate, Inc. World rights reserved. Reproduced by permission of North America Syndicate.

Preliminary Statistics for 2001 are similar. 140 of the nation's law enforcement officers were killed feloniously, including 71 in the terrorist attacks on September the 11th.

Firearms Help Protect Police

However, according to the NRA [National Rifle Association] Institute for Legislative Action, there have been 2.5 million protective uses of firearms every year in the United States. For many years, we have been telling the public to help us and to assist where they can. I have also seen a lot of talking heads on the news who try to convince people to "be alert and remain aware of your surroundings," when it comes to terrorism, but they can't seem to really be able to tell people what to do. Well, in my opinion, an armed citizenry already knows what to do. They protect themselves when we cannot.

Now, I am not arguing for vigilantism, but I am arguing that people need to take responsibility for themselves. We seem to be side stepping the issue when we speak about enemies of the United States and we are afraid to let law-abiding citizens protect themselves. The founding fathers of this country provided for the right to bear arms and I can think of no other time in history where it is more important to do so, than right now. As a police officer, I would actually feel safer knowing we had trained civilians who could help me when I needed it.

Pilots and Guns

It is better to have an armed pilot than to have to order a military plane to shoot down one of our own commercial airliners, full of innocent people, because hijackers have taken it over and are ready to do a repeat of last Sept. 11 [2001, when terrorists attacked]. . . .

Opponents of allowing pilots to be armed have portrayed horror movie visions of pilots and terrorists shooting it out in the aisles of airliners. But the main reason for arming pilots is not so that they can re-enact the gunfight at the OK corral. The main reason for having guns for self-defense anywhere is deterrence.

Thomas Sowell, "Pilots and Guns," *Capitalism Magazine*, July 27, 2002.

The only problem is that no one wants to say it. I trust the American people with weapons and I trust that they have the sense to know when or even if, to use them. Again according to the NRA, 32 States have a right to carry [RTC] law. On the average, crime rates in these states have lowered since the adoption of RTC. Out of all the protective uses of weapons in the U.S., only 1% of the weapon owners actually fired their weapon. With a little training in firearm safety, legal issues and shoot don't shoot we can have thousands more people on the street that can help us fight terrorism. It seems to me that the only people, who do not trust the people, is the politician. Imagine that.

"If guns are permitted in cars and in houses, they're all the more easily accessible for criminals, children and people in general who shouldn't have them in the first place."

Concealed Weapons Do Not Make Society Safer

Eric W. Alexy

In the following viewpoint Eric W. Alexy counters the claim by gun advocates that concealed weapons allow citizens to protect themselves from criminals. In reality, guns get into the wrong hands, he notes. Stolen from homes and cars by criminals, these guns end up used in violent crimes. He also asserts that allowing people to carry guns wherever they want will result in more gun deaths. Alexy is a contributing writer for the *Columbia Chronicle*.

As you read, consider the following questions:

1. As reported by the author, what are the criteria to get a permit to carry a concealed weapon in Missouri under the law passed in 2004?
2. For what kind of crimes were stolen guns used in recent years, as related by Alexy?
3. In the author's view, what is the ultimate solution to the problem of gun violence?

A fter a recent override in Missouri legislature, the state is set to see its right-to-carry laws go into effect Oct. 11 [2003]. Those wanting to carry a gun in Missouri must clear a background check, take a training course, pay $100 and be at least 23 years of age. Individuals with recent felonies, certain misdemeanors and/or mental disabilities are ineligible.

The most common argument heard from right-to-carry proponents is that guns are necessary for self-defense purposes. After all, murderers, rapists and robbers all seem to have guns, so let's even the playing field, they say.

Guns Get into the Wrong Hands

In a perfect world, guns would be used only for self-defense. In reality, however, guns get into the wrong hands, and people do bad things with them . . . very bad things, in fact. People who should never be able to own a gun in the first place occasionally slip through the cracks.

Under House Bill No. 349, those with permits will be able to bring their guns into public buildings—that is, buildings that don't post signs saying you can't bring guns into their facilities. (Shouldn't it be the other way around?) While you can't bring guns into government buildings, courthouses and police stations, according to the bill, stadiums with fewer than 5,000 seats are just fine.

That is where the newly enacted law oversteps self-defense into the territory of insanity.

It's understandable that one would want to have a gun in their home to fend off would-be intruders, but permitting guns into little league baseball games (assuming the game isn't at a school or church, two other no-goes) and the local K-Mart store lacks common sense, if not humanity.

Harmless Brawls Turn into Deadly Shootings

A drunken brawl at a baseball game ensues over an ump's call. At what point do you draw your gun in fear that the other guy will use his first? Same goes with road rage. A simple scuffle can take on a life of its own when (almost) anyone can carry a gun. As the saying goes, "kill or be killed."

The bottom line is that guns kill a lot more people than they save. How many gun deaths would there be if guns didn't exist at all? Or if mere possession of a gun landed someone a lengthy jail sentence? It would probably deter a lot of people from carrying guns, that's for sure.

American Attitudes About Concealed Weapons

Fifty-two percent want concealed-gun carrying to be limited to "people with a special need to carry a concealed gun, such as private detectives," and 46% favor allowing carry permits to "any adult who has passed a criminal background check and a gun safety course" (2.5% were missing or didn't have an opinion). These attitudes were examined further by asking people follow-up items that challenged their initial preference. When those favoring restricting concealed carrying to people with special needs were told that "this would mean that most law-abiding people could not carry concealed handguns even if they thought they needed to for self-protection," 82% still backed limiting concealed carrying to those with special needs, 14% switched to allowing concealed carrying for those passing a background check and a gun-safety course, and 3% were undecided. Those favoring general access to concealed-gun permits were told that "this would mean that anyone with a concealed-carry permit could bring handguns into stores and malls, restaurants and bars, and other public places." After hearing this 62% still backed general access, 33% now opposed this, and 6% were undecided. This indicates that opinions for limiting concealed carrying to those with special needs was firmer than attitudes in favor of more general access.

Tom W. Smith, *2001 National Gun Policy Survey of the National Opinion Research Center: Research Findings,* National Opinion Research Center, University of Chicago, Chicago, IL, 2001, pp. 3–4.

Logic is absent on many of the stats given on the National Rifle Association's Website, www.nra.org. One header on the site reads: "more right to carry states, less crime." However, it seems hard to believe that having more people with guns would deter crime. After all, if guns are permitted in cars and in houses, they're all the more easily accessible for criminals, children and people in general who shouldn't have them in the first place.

The gun may help you when it's by your side, but who's to stop someone from taking it when left unattended? And who's to say the bad guy wouldn't somehow take the gun from you when you did try to use it?

How many stolen guns are used every year to commit crimes? Lots. School shootings in Flint, Mich., and Springfield, Ore. occurred with weapons that were easily stolen. How many murders would have never happened if guns were much more difficult to obtain than they are right now?

Perhaps if everyone in America was of stable mind and temper, this wouldn't be an issue. But as long as bad guys exist—as long as bad guys have guns, which will be as long as they can steal them or buy them—people will feel the need to defend themselves with guns.

Get Rid of the Guns

Starting at the root of the problem, it would seem reasonable to get rid of all the guns currently in circulation, not permit the production of more of them.

The problem with guns seems to be the same as tobacco, booze and any other killer of thousands that makes billions: If it makes money, the likelihood of common sense taking precedence over dollar signs is close to nil, thus negating any chance of a nationwide ban on firearms ever happening.

Odds are that if all guns were slowly eliminated—banned, melted down, whatever—the problem with people dying from guns would eventually go away.

Eventually, cops wouldn't even need to carry guns. If guns were completely illegal, it would be a lot easier to tell which guy with a gun under the seat of his car or in his pants' pocket in line at the grocery store is a criminal: all of them.

"We cannot wait for another [school shooting] before we address how easy it is for criminals and terrorists to legally purchase these hand-held weapons of mass destruction."

Assault Weapons Increase the Threat of Gun Violence

Carolyn McCarthy

In the following viewpoint Carolyn McCarthy contends that a strict assault weapons ban is needed to protect police officers and the public from criminals, who buy the weapons to commit crimes. With the expiration of the old assault weapons ban in September 2004, she emphasizes the need to pass a new ban that prohibits the sale and possession of assault weapons. The ban was not reinstated as of 2005. McCarthy is a U.S. representative from Long Island, New York. In 1993 McCarthy's husband was killed in a shooting on the Long Island Railroad.

As you read, consider the following questions:
1. Does the public support the assault weapons ban, according to the author?
2. As cited by the author, do police organizations support an assault weapons ban?
3. How does McCarthy plan to improve on the assault weapons ban that expired in 2004?

Carolyn McCarthy, address to the U.S. House, Washington, DC, May 10, 2005.

Last Saturday's [May 7, 2005] *New York Times* revealed that since the expiration of the Federal ban on assault weapons there have been no real boom in sales of the weapons at American gun stores. Opponents of the ban seized the opportunity to say the ban was ineffective. However, I think these statistics prove that assault weapons have absolutely no practical purpose except to kill human beings.

Many Members of the House have told me the assault weapons ban is an affront on our second amendment rights, but the public never saw the assault weapons ban as an infringement on their second amendment rights. Last September [2004], a Dallas newspaper ran a poll indicating that 78 percent of Texas gun owners supported keeping the ban in place. And nobody takes their second amendment rights more seriously than Texas gun owners. So nobody should be surprised that the sales of these weapons are so low.

People Are Buying Assault Weapons

However, some people are buying these weapons. They may intend to use these guns in crimes; and because of our gun laws [enacted prior to the September 11, 2001, terrorist attacks], these people could possibly be aligned with our enemies in the war on terror. It is time for this Congress to finally be proactive when it comes to gun safety and gun laws. We cannot wait for another Columbine [school shooting] before we address how easy it is for criminals and terrorists to legally purchase these hand-held weapons of mass destruction.

We need commonsense gun laws that allow law-abiding citizens to purchase guns for sport and self-defense, but ensure that those criminals with felonies and terrorist backgrounds cannot arm themselves. We need a new stronger assault weapons ban.

One of the things that I certainly will be working for is the large-capacity clips.

Why Assault Weapons Are Dangerous

There are many that will say, Well, it doesn't matter how many clips you have. But if you see what these clips can do, especially against our police officers, it is something that we should not allow, certainly in this country. The only ones that should be allowed to own them are our police officers and certainly our military.

Resourceful criminals still found a way to obtain illegal weapons. However, the ban made these weapons more expensive. And because they became more expensive, we saw that gangs were not buying these guns. I think that is one of the reasons why it worked.

The Public Supports Renewing and Strengthening the Assault Weapons Ban

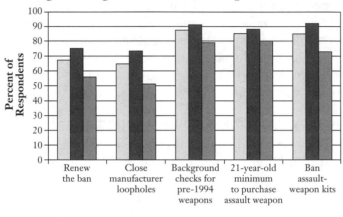

☐ All Respondents ■ Non–Gun Owners ■ Gun Owners

"Consumers Strongly Support Renewing and Strengthening the Federal Assault Weapons Ban," Consumer Federation of America, 2004.

Tomorrow [May 11, 2005] we are going to be voting on an anti-gang bill [bill has been referred to Senate committee]. We see our police officers on the front line against these gangs all the time. During the 10 years that the ban was in place, crimes involving banned weapons dropped by 60 percent, so we do know that it was working. Nearly every police organization in this country supported the assault weapons ban and wants to make sure that we try and get it in place again. When the men and women on the front lines in the war on gangs and crime in this country say they want assault weapons banned, we should listen.

This week we are celebrating or mourning those police officers that were killed in this last past year. Every year it seems that the numbers are growing. We should be doing more to protect our police officers that try to protect us on a daily basis. However, we need to improve on the shortfalls of the old ban, namely, [clips] as I have mentioned that hold more than 10 rounds.

Personally, I remember going back to 1993 when there was a shooting on the Long Island Railroad and my husband was one of those killed. The person that was doing the shooting had clips of 15 and more bullets. Every one of those bullets made its mark, killing a number of people and injuring many, my husband dying and my son certainly being injured. If we had a clip that was only 10, 15 people might not have been injured or killed. I think that is important.

Limiting Who Can Own Assault Weapons

The only Americans who should be allowed to have these weapons are soldiers and police officers, as I have said. Using one of these weapons with these clips in your home would certainly take down an intruder, but the bullets are flying. Come on, let us use some common sense. They would be flying all over the place. You could be hitting your neighbor. Why do we need clips that are more than 10? As I said, our police officers should have them, but it will probably be when we see these gangs buying the large-capacity clips, that is when we will have outrage here. . . .

It is time to stop listening to the NRA's [National Rifle Association's] rhetoric and start listening to common sense. We should be working together. The whole idea is to make sure that people are safe. No legislation that anyone is trying to do that I am aware of is taking away the right of someone to own a gun. We certainly should make it harder for those criminals, those terrorists that are out there at gun shows buying guns, criminals and gangs buying guns illegally. We can do a better job.

*"Despite the heated rhetoric, there is not
one single academic study showing that
these bans have reduced any type of
violent crime."*

Banning Assault Weapons Will Not Make Society Safer

John R. Lott Jr.

John R. Lott Jr. argues in the following viewpoint that the expiration of the assault weapons ban in September 2004 will not raise the rate of violent crime in the United States. According to Lott, guns called assault weapons are not fundamentally different from other kinds of arms. As of late 2005, there have been no successful attempts to reinstate an assault weapons ban. A resident scholar at the American Enterprise Institute, Lott is a well-known gun advocate.

As you read, consider the following questions:

1. According to the author, what did John Kerry say about assault weapons?
2. What are the similarities between fully automatic assault weapons and semiautomatic hunting weapons, in the author's view?
3. Why have gun control organizations backed off on their support of the assault weapons ban, as stated by Lott?

D o you feel more fearful today then yesterday? Gun control advocates apparently do, but not for the reason that most people think.

At the midnight just passed [in 2004], the federal "assault weapons" ban expired. [As of 2005, it has not been reinstated.]

Despite claims that allowing the ban on some semiautomatic weapons to end will cause a rise in gun crimes and a surge in police killings, letting the law expire will show the uselessness of gun-control regulations and the inconveniences they cause.

The Horror Stories Are Wrong

Very soon it will be obvious to everyone that all the horror stories that were used to make the case for the ban—one of the two major gun control regulations over the last 36 years —were wrong.

The risks Americans wake up to Tuesday are being portrayed as deadly serious. Sarah Brady, a leading gun control advocate, warns that "Our streets are going to be filled with AK47s and Uzis."

Ratcheting up the fear factor to an entirely new level, Sen. John Kerry finally entered the fray Friday by claiming that sunsetting the ban makes "the job of terrorists easier."

Despite the heated rhetoric, there is not one single academic study showing that these bans have reduced any type of violent crime. Even research funded by the Justice Department under the Clinton administration concluded that the ban's "impact on gun violence has been uncertain."

Gun Laws Do Not Help

When those same authors released their revised report in August looking at crime data up through 2000, the first six full years of the law, they claimed: "We cannot clearly credit the ban with any of the nation's recent drop in gun violence."

My own research examining crime data from 1977 through 1998 also found no reductions in any type of violent crime from either the state or federal laws. The law's only effect was to reduce gun shows by about 20%.

The explanation for these findings is very simple: There is nothing unique about the guns that were banned.

While the "assault weapons" ban conjures up images of machine guns used by the military, the guts of these guns are the same as any semiautomatic hunting rifle. They fire the same bullets with the same rapidity and produce the same damage as hunting rifles.

The Definition of Assault Weapons

A *genuine* assault weapon, as opposed to a legal definition, is a hand-held, selective fire weapon, which means it's capable of firing in either an automatic or a semiautomatic mode depending on the position of a selector switch. These kinds of weapons are heavily regulated by the National Firearms Act of 1934 and are further regulated in some states.

However, current "assault weapon" legislation defines certain semi-automatic weapons as "assault weapons." A semi-automatic weapon is one that fires a round with each pull of the trigger, versus an automatic weapon which continues to shoot until the trigger is released or the ammunition supply is exhausted. These kinds of "assault weapons" are sometimes referred to as military-style semi-automatic weapons.

An example of assault weapon legislation is the Federal 1994 Crime Bill. The bill in part outlaws new civilian manufacture of certain semi-automatic assault weapons. It also prohibits new civilian manufacture of "large capacity ammunition feeding devices" declared certain weapons as assault weapons, and states a semiautomatic *rifle* is an assault weapon if it can accept a detachable magazine and has two or more of the following:

- A folding or telescoping stock
- A pistol grip
- A bayonet mount
- A flash suppressor, or threads to attach one
- A grenade launcher.

"Assault Weapons," GunCite.com, March 1, 2005. www.guncite.com.

When Sarah Brady talks about "AK-47s and Uzis" flooding the streets or Kerry says "I never contemplated hunting deer or anything else with an AK-47," people unfortunately think they are referring to the guns actually used by militaries, not their civilian knockoffs.

The firing mechanisms in semiautomatic and fully automatic machine guns are completely different. The entire firing mechanism of a semiautomatic gun has to be gutted and replaced to turn it into a machine gun. The term "military style" is tossed around in the media, but the key word is "style."

Surprisingly, it is now not just gun control opponents making this argument. Some gun-control groups, such as the Violence Policy Center, also began changing course last spring [2004], a week after the renewal was defeated in the Senate. Despite spending a decade claiming it was a "myth" that "assault weapons merely look different," a Violence Policy Center spokesperson now claims:

"If the existing assault-weapons ban expires, I personally do not believe it will make one whit of difference one way or another in terms of our objective, which is reducing death and injury and getting a particularly lethal class of firearms off the streets. So if it doesn't pass, it doesn't pass."

Credibility Problem

As National Public Radio reported: "(The Violence Policy Center's representative) says that's all the (assault weapons ban) brought about—minor changes in appearance that didn't alter the function of these weapons."

It is hard to believe this is the same gun-control organization responsible for the widely reported claim that the ban protected police.

So why the sudden conversion? Why wait until a week after the fiercely fought renewal was defeated in the Senate before suddenly morphing into Gilda Radner's *Saturday Night Live* character Emily Litella saying "never mind"?

To put it simply, gun-control groups' credibility is on the line. When it will be obvious to everyone in just months that all the horror stories about banning what have been labeled "assault weapons" were wrong, they want to try to claim they didn't think the law ever really mattered.

Regulations rarely seem to disappear, especially ones with this much hype behind them. The media will undoubtedly try to keep the debate alive by focusing on particular crimes whenever a previously banned gun is used. But it will be harder to take gun control claims seriously in the future.

Still, it would have been nice if gun-control organizations had been honest and told us all this a decade ago.

Periodical Bibliography

The following articles have been selected to supplement the diverse views presented in this chapter.

Jordan Carleo-Evangelist	"Guns and Crime: The Great Debate," *Albany Times Union*, October 18, 2004.
Ed Cohen	"Public Enemy No. 1," *Notre Dame Magazine*, Winter 2000.
Gene Healy	"Less Guns, More Crime," *American Spectator*, January 20, 2004.
Bronwyn Jones	"Arming Myself with a Gun Is Not the Answer," *Newsweek*, May 22, 2000.
Dave Kopel	"Bait-n-Switch," *National Review Online*, September 13, 2004. www.nationalreview.com.
Dave Kopel	"Brothers in Arms," *Reason*, February 24, 2005.
John R. Lott Jr.	"Half-Cocked: Why Most of What You See in the Media About Guns Is Wrong," *American Enterprise*, July 1, 2003.
John R. Lott Jr.	"The Big Lie of the Assault Weapons Ban," *Los Angeles Times*, June 28, 2005.
Carlisle E. Moody and Thomas Marvell	"Guns and Crime," *Southern Economic Journal*, April 2005.
Jonathan Rauch	"And Don't Forget Your Gun," *National Journal*, March 20, 1999.
Alec Rawls	"Blacks and Guns," *Capitalism Magazine*, January 26, 2003.
Paul Craig Roberts	"Guns and Violence," *Townhall.com*, July 29, 2002. www.townhall.com.

CHAPTER 3

Does the Constitution Protect Private Gun Ownership?

Chapter Preface

Central to the gun control debate is the Second Amendment of the U.S. Constitution, which provides that "a well regulated Militia, being necessary to the security of a free State, the right of the people to keep and bear Arms, shall not be infringed." Debate has raged for years over whether the right to bear arms represents an "individual" or "collective" right. Gun rights activists argue that the Second Amendment refers to an individual right, which grants citizens the right to use guns for lawful purposes. On the other side, gun control activists contend that the Second Amendment defines a collective right, protecting the states' authority to create and maintain organized militias.

Federal courts have generally come down on the side of the collective rights argument. In 1939 a legal precedent was set in *United States v. Miller*, in which the U.S. Supreme Court ruled that the Second Amendment did not protect an individual's right to own a shotgun because such a right did not have a "reasonable relationship to the preservation or efficiency of a well regulated militia." Since the *Miller* decision, virtually every lower court has accepted the collective rights interpretation of the Second Amendment—that is, until *United States v. Emerson* (1998). In this case Timothy Emerson was charged with violating the Lautenberg Amendment to the 1994 Gun Act, which prohibits possession of a firearm by persons under a domestic violence restraining order. He was tried in district court, where Emerson's lawyers argued that his case should be dismissed on the grounds that the federal ban on gun possession by those under a protective order for domestic violence violated the Second Amendment. The district judge sided with Emerson and dismissed the charges. However, the U.S. Justice Department then appealed the trial court's decision, stating that it directly conflicted with long-established legal precedent laid down by the U.S. Supreme Court in *Miller*.

When the Fifth Circuit Court of Appeals reversed the lower court decision and upheld the domestic violence gun ban, gun control advocates viewed the decision as a victory for domestic violence victims. Gun rights advocates also claimed a victory, however, as the decision seemed to affirm an individual rights interpretation of the Second Amendment. Although the court had supported a restriction on Timothy Emerson's right to own a gun because of his violent tendencies, the court had also found that individual, law-abiding Americans are guaranteed the right to own a gun under the Second Amendment. With legal precedent on both sides, the debate still rages over the meaning of the Second Amendment.

*"Congress now has a historic opportunity,
not simply to stave off new gun-control
proposals, but to begin restoring
Americans' right to keep and bear arms."*

The Second Amendment Protects Private Gun Ownership

Cato Institute

In the following viewpoint writers from the Cato Institute argue that in recent years American courts have interpreted the Second Amendment as protecting the right of individuals to own guns. The authors further contend that the amendment's placement in the Bill of Rights—in the section devoted to individual, not state, rights—proves that its protection applies to individual citizens, not just militias. The Cato Institute is a nonprofit, libertarian public policy research foundation headquartered in Washington, D.C.

As you read, consider the following questions:

1. What did the 2001 *United States v. Emerson* decision say about the Second Amendment?
2. How did the U.S. Justice Department react to the *United States v. Emerson* decision?
3. How did American citizens protect themselves in the 1700s, according to the authors?

For decades, the Second Amendment was consigned to constitutional exile, all but erased from constitutional law textbooks and effectively banished from the nation's courts. But no more. Recent developments in the law and in political culture have begun the process of returning the amendment to its proper place in our constitutional pantheon. Congress now has a historic opportunity, not simply to stave off new gun-control proposals, but to begin restoring Americans' right to keep and bear arms.

Understanding the Second Amendment

Ideas have consequences, and so does constitutional text. Though elite opinion reduced the Second Amendment to a constitutional inkblot for a good part of the 20th century, gun enthusiasts and grassroots activists continued to insist that the amendment meant what it said. And slowly, often reluctantly, legal scholars began to realize that the activists were right. Liberal law professor Sanford Levinson conceded as much in a 1989 *Yale Law Journal* article titled "The Embarrassing Second Amendment." UCLA Law School's Eugene Volokh took a similar intellectual journey. After a 1990 argument with a nonlawyer acquaintance who loudly maintained that the Second Amendment protected an individual right, Volokh concluded that his opponent was a "blowhard and even a bit of a kook." But several years later, as he researched the subject, he discovered to his "surprise and mild chagrin, that this supposed kook was entirely right": the amendment secures the individual's right to keep and bear arms. That's also what the Fifth Circuit Court of Appeals concluded in October 2001 when it decided *United States v. Emerson*. It held that the Constitution "protects the right of individuals, including those not then actually a member of any militia . . . to privately possess and bear their own firearms . . . that are suitable as personal individual weapons."

U.S. Attorney General John Ashcroft has endorsed the *Emerson* court's reading of the amendment. First, in a letter to the National Rifle Association, Ashcroft stated his belief that "the text and the original intent of the Second Amendment clearly protect the right of individuals to keep and bear firearms." That letter was followed by Justice Department briefs before the Supreme Court in the *Emerson* case and in *United States v. Haney.* For the first time, the federal government argued in formal court papers that the "Second Amendment . . . protects the rights of individuals, including persons who are not members of any militia . . . to possess and bear their own firearms, subject to reasonable restrictions designed to prevent possession by unfit persons or . . . firearms that are particularly suited to criminal misuse."

The Right of the People

What's driving the new consensus? Let's look at the amendment's text: "A well regulated Militia, being necessary to the security of a free State, the right of the people to keep and bear Arms, shall not be infringed." The operative clause ("the right of the people to keep and bear Arms, shall not be infringed") secures the right. The explanatory clause ("A well regulated Militia, being necessary to the security of a free State") justifies the right. That syntax was not unusual for the times. For example, the free press clause of the 1842 Rhode Island Constitution states: "The liberty of the press being essential to the security of freedom in a state, any person may publish his sentiments of any subject." That provision surely does not mean that the right to publish protects only the press. It protects "any person"; and one reason among others that it protects any person is that a free press is essential to a free society. Analogously, the Second Amendment protects "the people"; and one reason among others that it protects the people is that it ensures a well-regulated militia. As George Mason University law professor Nelson Lund puts it, imagine if the Second Amendment said, "A well-educated Electorate, being necessary to self-governance in a free state, the right of the people to keep and read Books shall not be infringed." Surely, no rational person would suggest that only registered voters have a right to read. Yet that is precisely the effect if the text is interpreted to apply only to a well-educated electorate. Analogously, the Second Amendment cannot be read to apply only to members of the militia.

The Second Amendment, like the First and the Fourth, refers explicitly to "the right of the people." Consider the placement of the amendment within the Bill of Rights, the

The Second Amendment Protects Our Rights

The prime purpose behind the writing of the Second Amendment of the *Bill of Rights* was not only to guard against invasion from *without*, but primarily to guard against the invasion of the people's liberty from *within*. When public officials prohibit or obstruct the right to arms held by the people, and interfere with the citizen's use of arms necessary for the prevention of tyranny in government, that legislation is called sedition.

Second Amendment Committee, "The Second Amendment Is an Absolute Right," 2005.

part of the Constitution that deals exclusively with rights of individuals, not powers of the state. No one can doubt that First Amendment rights (speech, religion, assembly) belong to us as individuals. Similarly, Fourth Amendment protections against unreasonable searches and seizures are individual rights. In the context of the Second Amendment, we secure "the right of the people" by guaranteeing the right of each person. Second Amendment protections are not for the state but for each individual against the state—a deterrent to government tyranny.

Protection Against Criminal Predators

And not just against government tyranny. The Second Amendment also secures our right to protect ourselves from criminal predators. After all, in 1791 there were no organized, professional police forces to speak of in America. Self-defense was the responsibility of the individual and the community and not, in the first instance, of the state. Armed citizens, responsibly exercising their right of self-defense, are an effective deterrent to crime.

Today, states' incompetence at defending citizens against criminals is a more palpable threat to our liberties than is tyranny by the state. But that incompetence coupled with a disarmed citizenry could well create the conditions that lead to tyranny. The demand for police to defend us increases in proportion to our inability to defend ourselves. That's why disarmed societies tend to become police states. Witness law-abiding inner-city residents, many of whom have been disarmed by gun control, begging for police protection against drug gangs—despite the terrible violations of civil liberties, such as curfews and anti-loitering laws, that such protection entails. The right to bear arms is thus preventive—it reduces the demand for a police state. George Washington University law professor Robert Cottrol put it this way: "A people incapable of protecting themselves will lose their rights as a free people, becoming either servile dependents of the state or of the criminal predators."

"When it comes to military matters (and the Second Amendment is undeniably and exclusively about that) individualism loses to organization and discipline hands down."

The Second Amendment Does Not Protect Private Gun Ownership

Barry S. Willdorf

In the following viewpoint Barry S. Willdorf maintains that the Second Amendment applies to states' rights to bear arms, not to the rights of individuals. He asserts that the amendment's wording, which says that the maintenance of a militia is necessary for the security of a free state, makes clear that it grants the right to own guns to the states, not to individuals. Willdorf is a civil rights activist and trial attorney living in San Francisco, California.

As you read, consider the following questions:

1. According to the author's description, what is the difference in the gun culture between New Zealand and the United States?
2. How do people who believe in the individual rights interpretation of the Second Amendment misinterpret it, in the author's view?
3. In Willdorf's opinion, how does a collective interpretation of the Second Amendment preserve American freedoms?

Not long ago, I was stopped for exceeding the speed limit by about 10 mph. It was on a nearly deserted two-lane country road, straight as a yardstick. A gentleman in a lime green vest stepped into the middle of the road beside an ordinary looking Ford. He was unarmed.

"The officer in the car behind you would like to have a word with you, sir," he said politely, when I pulled over.

I looked in my rear view mirror and indeed there was another ordinary looking Ford pulling in behind me. When I looked up again, the first officer had departed, leaving me alone with the second cop.

He casually exited his vehicle and donned his own lime green vest. He too was unarmed. He walked up to my window. "Do you know how fast you were going, sir?" he asked.

"I had you clocked at 113," he told me, when I shook my head. "That's thirteen kph over the limit. We have a 10 kph grace here and you exceeded it. I'm afraid I'll have to give you a summons. There are no exceptions. Please blow into this, sir," he told me. "We are required to give everyone we stop a breathalyzer."

After I passed it, he asked to see my license. "Ah, you're an American," he said with a smile. "Can I see your passport?"

"It's in my backpack, in the back seat," I explained. "Can I get out of the car and get it?"

The officer stood back a few steps to permit me open the door. "It's all right," he replied. "We don't shoot you here."

Incredibly, he permitted me to rummage through my backpack. After I gave him my passport and he gave me my ticket, he also provided my wife and me with more local tourist information than we really wanted to know, or had time to see. "There's a fine lake just a short drive away," he mentioned with a wink as he was leaving. "The tourists don't know about it, but I wouldn't miss it if I were you." He removed his lime green vest, got back into his vehicle and reset his speed trap.

The entire experience was unthinkable in terms of American police procedure. It can only be explained by the difference in gun culture that exists between America and New Zealand. If we use guns as the criteria, on the civilization spectrum we seem to be as far apart as we are geographically.

New Zealand Gun Culture

That is not to say that guns are unknown to New Zealanders. Hunting there is a popular sporting activity. New Zealanders contend, person for person that they are among the best shots in the world. Nearly every town we visited has a local rifle range and on a Saturday, when we drove past one, it seemed to be heavily in use by shooting enthusiasts.

Collective Right Interpretation Under Siege

Through a statistical analysis of Second Amendment writings based on the *Index to Legal Periodicals*, [political scientist Robert] Spitzer discovered that from 1912 to 1999 there have been 76 substantive articles in legal journals defending the collective-rights view and 88 supporting the "individualist" view. It looks as though the contesting interpretations are running pretty much neck and neck—until you examine the interval between 1990 and 1999. That period witnessed the publication of 58 of the 88 total Ashcroftian-interpretation individualist articles; 79 out of 88 have been written since 1980. Based on Spitzer's numbers, it does look as though a "preponderance of legal scholarship" has very recently coalesced behind [former attorney general John] Ashcroft's view.

Chris Mooney, "Standard Shift," *The American Prospect Online*, August 13, 2001.

To obtain the right to keep a firearm in a home in New Zealand, an applicant must prove that he or she is knowledgeable in the use, maintenance and care of the weapon. He or she must pass an extensive background check that involves proving that the gun will be kept locked in a safe and secure location. The applicant's spouse or domestic partner is interviewed in private to determine whether he or she agrees that the weapon can be kept at the home and that he or she does not feel threatened in any way. And that applies to long guns: rifles and shotguns. It is illegal for a private citizen, even a police officer to keep a handgun in the home or office. Handguns have to be kept in approved firing ranges.

Can this happen here? The other day, the Sunday paper was filled with memorials to San Francisco Police Officer Isaac Espinoza, gunned down in the city's Bayview District, a tiny enclave where gun-related murders annually far exceed those in the entire country of New Zealand. At the same time, the paper also related how two notoriously right-leaning fundamentalist politicians were re-evaluating their support for the death penalty, citing the "culture of life." Change can happen. It doesn't happen by fiat, though. It happens by convincing people that there is a better alternative.

Perhaps I am going out on a limb here, but I would venture the opinion that most people, including most police, would prefer the New Zealand model of a relationship with guns. How do we get there?

Reading the Second Amendment

I think that we have to start with clearing up a really big misunderstanding about the Second Amendment. The Second Amendment to the U.S. Constitution states: "A well regulated Militia, being necessary to the security of a free State, the right of the people to keep and bear arms, shall not be infringed."

It is critical to bear in mind that in addition to reference to a militia, the Second Amendment also specifically mentions a "free State." For more than 150 years, this has been interpreted to mean that the decisions on how to regulate the keeping and bearing of arms must be made at the state level, unless the people of the state, as a whole, grant such rights to political subdivisions. To conclude otherwise would, in effect allow every individual, city, town and county to opt out of its obligation to participate in a well-regulated militia. In this regard, doubters should note that §129 of the California Military and Veteran's Code provides that failure to keep and bear arms as commanded by the governor is deemed desertion.

On the other hand, the Second Amendment says nothing about hunting. Nor does it mention the right of the people to fend off burglars or robbers by the use of guns in self-defense. Our founding fathers were fluent with the English language. The words "hunt," "burglar," "robber" and "self-defense" all were then in common usage. They were not used. From this simple fact we can conclude that when contemporary politicians talk about their love of hunting or the need for their use to protect homeowners from burglars in the context of gun owner rights, we know that they are evading the issue. They are being dishonest. Quite frankly, so is the NRA [National Rifle Association].

The Second Amendment is not the only place that the U.S. Constitution mentions militias. The states' rights regarding militias are set forth in the body of the Constitution, Article 1, Section 8, Clause 15, that gives Congress the power to call up the states' militias to execute the laws of the union, to suppress insurrections, and repel invasions. Clause 16 gives Congress the power to organize, arm, and discipline the militia but then provides that the states have the right to appoint the officers of the militia and the authority to train it.

The Courts Confirm It

One of the most hotly debated issues of constitutional interpretation and application is whether the Second Amendment confers rights to private citizens to own and/or bear firearms. Exhaustive research of well-settled case law answers the question, "No!"

From the middle of the 19th century to the present, a consistent line of Supreme Court and federal appellate court decisions holds that the amendment does not concern private citizens.

Robert Simmons, *San Diego Union-Tribune*, January 27, 1997.

The Second Amendment modified Congress' power by reserving to the people the ultimate right to arm themselves as part of a militia. If Congress fails or refuses to arm the militia, the people have the right to do it through their state government, in such manner as they decide is most fitting.

Thus there can be little doubt that the right reserved to us in the Second Amendment has to do only with assisting us in preserving our other freedoms, collectively in a well-regulated state militia. That is the only reason we have the right granted to us in the Second Amendment. How we, as a free people, decide to regulate ourselves is our choice.

Our Collective Freedom

Because it is all about preserving our collective freedom, it is not constitutionally an individual right, unless we, as a people, want it to be that way. This means that the people collectively can regulate the right of an individual to keep and bear arms in the interests of preserving their freedom. To contend that the keeping or bearing of arms is an individual right actually impedes our right to make rules concerning firearms that in our collective judgment are most likely to preserve our freedom.

We, as a democratic people must not be prevented from regulating the keeping and bearing of arms in such a manner as we agree will be most likely to protect our free state. The alternative interpretation, granting each individual the right to keep and bear arms in an unregulated manner, rather than facilitating the preservation of a free state, invites anarchy and puts our freedom at risk.

Those readers who have had experience in the military know that when it comes to the keeping and bearing of arms, it is far more restrictive that the most restrictive of states. Except in combat situations, soldiers may not keep and bear arms among their personal gear. When not being used for training, weapons are maintained in armories or under lock. Ammunition is accounted for. Each weapon is signed for and the signatory is strictly accountable for it.

The Second Amendment does not compel that the rules with respect to civilians be more lax. Viewed in this way, we must conclude that the Second Amendment poses no bar to the reasonable regulation of firearms by state governments. Indeed, so interpreted, it facilitates the effective preservation of our freedoms.

One has only to travel through the towns and villages of New Zealand, observing the many memorials to their fallen to know that they can demonstrate a history of success with firearms regulation that is harmonious with my interpretation of the Second Amendment. No one can doubt that they have been able to muster their forces when needed to preserve their freedom. Nor can it be disputed that their ability to defend their country has been hampered because they are prohibited from stashing a handgun in the glove compartment of their pickup.

While we, as Americans, are justifiably proud of our individualism, no one can rationally dispute that when it comes to military matters (and the Second Amendment is undeniably and exclusively about that) individualism loses to organization and discipline hands down. It is the ironic fact that to preserve our individual freedoms we sometimes must put them aside and demand collective discipline. Guns are one of those issues where that reality just has to be accepted. In exchange, we can have traffic stops where the cops don't shoot us. I call that a pretty fair trade.

"It is time for the American people to know the truth about the Second Amendment and for the NRA's systematic distortion of our Constitution to stop."

Gun Control Is Constitutional

Brady Center to Prevent Gun Violence

The Brady Center to Prevent Gun Violence maintains in the following viewpoint that U.S. courts have established that the Second Amendment protects states'—not individuals'—right to bear arms. Therefore, the center asserts, restrictions on private gun ownership do not violate Second Amendment rights. The Brady Center is one of the leading gun control organizations in the United States.

As you read, consider the following questions:

1. How many Americans are killed by guns every day, as cited by the center?
2. According to the Brady Center, how does the NRA misinterpret the Second Amendment?
3. What is the concept of a "well-regulated militia," in the author's view?

Brady Center to Prevent Gun Violence "The Second Amendment Myth and Meaning," The Legal Action Project, 2005. Copyright © 2005 by the Brady Campaign to Prevent Gun Violence. Reproduced by permission.

The Second Amendment to the United States Constitution: "A well regulated Militia, being necessary to the security of a free State, the right of the people to keep and bear Arms, shall not be infringed."

The NRA's Second Amendment Myth

Our nation suffers from an epidemic of gun violence. Guns take the lives of 105 Americans every day—15 of them are children and teenagers. In the four years between 1988 and 1991, more Americans were murdered with firearms than were killed in battle during the eight years of the Vietnam War. Sensible national gun control laws are urgently needed to stem this violence.

Time and time again, the National Rifle Association and other opponents of rational restrictions on guns charge that gun control laws violate the Second Amendment to our Constitution. According to the NRA, the Second Amendment's guarantee of a "right to keep and bear arms" is as broad and fundamental as the First Amendment freedoms of speech, assembly and the press. The NRA has even argued that citizens have a constitutional right to own machine guns and military-style assault weapons!

The NRA's constitutional theory is a calculated distortion of the text, history and judicial interpretation of the Second Amendment. In the words of former U.S. Supreme Court Chief Justice Warren Burger, the NRA has perpetrated a "fraud on the American public."

Contrary to the gun lobby's propaganda, the Second Amendment guarantees the people the right to be armed *only in connection with service in a "well regulated Militia."* Courts consistently have ruled that there is no constitutional right to own a gun for private purposes unrelated to the organized state militia.

It is time for the debate over gun violence to focus on the real issues, free from the NRA's constitutional mythology.

The Text of the Second Amendment

The gun lobby's distortion of the Second Amendment begins with its words. How many times have you heard an opponent of gun control cite the "right to keep and bear arms" without mentioning the introductory phrase "A well regulated Militia, being necessary to the security of a free State . . ."? In fact, some years ago, when the NRA placed the words of the Second Amendment near the front door of its national headquarters in Washington, D.C., it omitted that phrase entirely!

The NRA's convenient editing is not surprising; the omitted phrase is the key to understanding that the Second Amendment guarantees only a limited right that is not violated by laws affecting the private ownership of firearms.

The "obvious purpose" of the Second Amendment was "to assure the continuation and render possible the effectiveness" of state militia forces.

"It must be interpreted and applied with that end in view."

—United States Supreme Court in
U.S. v. Miller, 307 U.S. 174 (1939)

The Original Intent

The concept of a "well regulated Militia" is somewhat foreign to 20th century America, but it is central to the meaning of the Second Amendment.

At the time the U.S. Constitution was adopted, each of the states had its own "militia"—a military force comprised of ordinary citizens serving as part-time soldiers. Most of the adult male population was required by state law to enlist in the militia. The militia was "well regulated" in the sense that its members were subject to various legal requirements. They were, for example, required to report for training several days a year, to supply their own equipment for militia use, including guns and horses, and sometimes to engage in military exercises away from home.

The purpose of the militia was expressed in the Second Amendment—to assure "the security of a free State"—against threats from without (e.g. invasions) and threats from within (e.g. rebellions, riots, etc.).

The "militia" was not, as some gun control opponents have claimed, simply another word for the armed citizenry. It was an *organized* military force, "well regulated" by the state governments. Noah Webster's Dictionary of 1828 defines "militia" as: ". . . the able bodied men organized into companies, regiments and brigades, with officers of all grades, and required by law to attend military exercises on certain days only, but at other times left to pursue their usual occupations."

When the Constitution was sent to the states for ratification in 1787, the continued viability of the state militia was a central issue. The new Constitution established a permanent army composed of professional soldiers and controlled by the federal government. The "Anti-Federalists," who sought changes in the newly proposed Constitution, were fearful of the federal standing army authorized by the Constitution. The use of troops by George III as an instrument of oppression was still fresh in their memories.

A Collective Right

We believe that the constitutional right to bear arms is primarily a collective one, intended mainly to protect the right of the states to maintain militias to assure their own freedom and security against the central government. In today's world, that idea is somewhat anachronistic and in any case would require weapons much more powerful than handguns or hunting rifles. The ACLU therefore believes that the Second Amendment does not confer an unlimited right upon individuals to own guns or other weapons nor does it prohibit reasonable regulation of gun ownership, such as licensing and registration.

American Civil Liberties Union, "Gun Control," March 4, 2002.

The Anti-Federalists saw the state militia as an effective counterpoint to the power of the standing army but they were concerned that the federal government had excessive power over the militia. They argued that the Constitution left the arming of the state militia exclusively to the federal government. During the Virginia ratification debates, Patrick Henry asked: "When this power is given to Congress without limits or boundary, how will your militia be armed?"

The Second Amendment was written in response to this Anti-Federalist concern. The Amendment affirms that the keeping and bearing of arms in a "well regulated Militia" of the states is a "right of the people," not dependent on the whim of the federal government. The original intent of the Second Amendment, therefore, was to prevent the federal government from passing laws that would disarm the state militia.

The Second Amendment in the Twentieth Century

The Second Amendment has become an anachronism, largely because of drastic changes in the militia it was designed to protect. We no longer have a citizen militia in which a large portion of the population is enrolled for part-time military service and required by the government to maintain private arms for such service. As the nation grew, it became unworkable and unduly expensive for the states to impose military training and service on that many Americans.

The modern "well regulated Militia" is the National Guard —a state-organized military force of ordinary citizens serving as part-time soldiers, like the early state militia. However, unlike the early militia, the National Guard is of more limited membership and depends on government-supplied—not privately owned—arms. Whereas in 1787 federal restrictions on privately owned guns may have interfered with the "well regulated Militia," this is not the case today. Gun control laws have no effect on the arming of today's militia, since those laws invariably exempt the National Guard. Therefore, they raise no serious Second Amendment issue.

> *"The purpose of the Second Amendment is to restrain the federal government from regulating the possession of arms where such regulation would interfere with the preservation or efficiency of the militia."*
>
> —U.S. v. Hale, 978 F 2d 1016 (8th Cir. 1992)

The Second Amendment in the Courts

As a matter of law, the meaning of the Second Amendment has been settled since the ruling of the U.S. Supreme Court in *U.S. v. Miller* (1939). In that case, the High Court wrote that the "obvious purpose" of the Second Amendment was "to assure the continuation and render possible the effectiveness" of the state militia. The Court added that the Amendment "must be interpreted and applied with that end in view." Since *Miller*, the Supreme Court has addressed the Second Amendment in two cases. In *Burton v. Sills* (1969), the Court dismissed the appeal of a state court ruling upholding New Jersey's strict gun control law, finding the appeal failed to present a "substantial federal question." And in *Lewis v. United States* (1980), the Court upheld the federal law banning felons from possessing guns. The Court found no "constitutionally protected liberties" infringed by the federal law.

In addition, in *Maryland v. United States* (1965) and *Perpich v. Department of Defense* (1990), cases not involving the Second Amendment, the Supreme Court has affirmed that today's militia is the National Guard.

Since *Miller* was decided, lower federal and state courts have addressed the meaning of the Second Amendment in more than thirty cases. In every case, the courts have decided that the Amendment guarantees a right to be armed only in connection with service in a "well regulated Militia." The courts unanimously have rejected the NRA's view that the Second Amendment is about the self-defense or sporting uses of guns. As the U.S. Court of Appeals for the Eighth Circuit wrote, the courts "have analyzed the Second Amendment purely in terms of protecting state militias, rather than individual rights." *United States v. Nelson* (1988).

The Second Amendment and the Gun Control Debate

The National Rifle Association spends millions of dollars every year to foster its myth that the Second Amendment guarantees a broad, individual right to be armed that precludes virtually every restriction on private ownership of guns. The gun lobby's efforts have had a profound influence on the gun control debate. Public opinion polls show that, although more than 60% of Americans erroneously believe that the Constitution gives them a right to be armed, only a minority of Americans believe that it should grant that right. It is time for the American people to know the truth about the Second Amendment and for the NRA's systematic distortion of our Constitution to stop.

As former Harvard Law School Dean Erwin Griswold put it, "to assert that the Constitution is a barrier to reasonable gun laws, in the face of the unanimous judgment of the federal courts to the contrary, exceeds the limits of principled advocacy. It is time for the NRA and its followers in Congress to stop trying to twist the Second Amendment from a reasoned (if antiquated) empowerment for a militia into a bulletproof personal right for anyone to wield deadly weaponry beyond legislative control."

"It's about time the citizens realized that what they are doing is abiding by unconstitutional laws that infringe on their rights."

Gun Control Is Unconstitutional

Dorothy Anne Seese

According to Dorothy Anne Seese in the following viewpoint, America's courts have distorted the true meaning of the Bill of Rights by enlarging the power of government and infringing on the rights of citizens. Numerous court decisions, for example, have upheld gun control laws as constitutional, she maintains. However, according to Seese, individuals' right to bear arms is guaranteed by the Second Amendment, and any law infringing on that right is unconstitutional. Seese is a freelance writer.

As you read, consider the following questions:
1. According to the author, what should be the role of the federal government?
2. In the author's view, what is the ultimate purpose of gun control laws?
3. What is American citizens' duty under the Bill of Rights, according to Seese?

Go ahead and dig out the Bill of Rights. If you don't have one at your desk, it's easy to locate on the internet. Just as the First Amendment has been bent, twisted and contorted by judicial opinions unfit for the America of the Founders, so the Second Amendment has suffered like torture from judicial decisions and "opinions" from courts based on the bias of the judge rather than the plain letter of the law. This is what the Second Amendment says:

A well-regulated militia, being necessary to the security of a free State, the right of the people to keep and bear arms, shall not be infringed.

The Security of a Free State

Notice that the emphasis or rationale for unfettered gun ownership is the security of a free state. The Founders did not form a "more perfect union" in the sense of a conformed, welded and unseverable Union, but a unity of purpose where the states were the sovereign entities and the federal government was highly limited in its duties and powers. All the Founders had to do to get a new "union" of unfettered central power was either continue as subjects of the Crown or make a new monarchy. Instead, they framed a federal republic (which is not a democracy) and the intent was for each state to have the allegiance of its citizens. We are called the "United States of America" because our forefathers agreed to unite as sovereign states with a common name, coinage, postal service, and certain executive and legislative powers enumerated in the Constitution, Bill of Rights and the several successive amendments. The concept of a strong central government was fostered and facilitated at the expense of over half a million lives during the war between the states.

Now if groups band together under a title "militia" they are immediately branded as insurrectionists, rebels, Nazis, skinheads, terrorists or some other fearsome title. Yet what they do is fully constitutional unless they break some other law, which may also be unconstitutional. That does not mean criminals are free to run loose in the streets. Indeed, before this "gun control" flap initiated by the globalists and enemies of a Free America began to enforce its agenda, people were expected to own guns for the protection of themselves and their property. Life and property were held as Values One and Two, respectively. In Arizona, once a wild west territory, it is now illegal to use lethal force to protect property, and difficult to use to save one's life. Arizona is now a disaster area of liberal thought and open borders, number one in violent crime.

The forces, governmental and non-governmental, that want to take away the guns of the citizens or "register" them are marching in lockstep with the forces that are taking away our right to use land freely, transferring it at will to "heritage lands" under the United Nations. Did you, citizens, authorize the government to give our land to the UN? No? How did it happen? It happened because most of what the federal government does has nothing to do with your rights under the Bill of Rights or our Constitution of free and sovereign states in a voluntary union as a nation.

Why this emphasis on guns? Let me tell you from my email—because this government has gone so far afield from the framework of the founders and the powers delegated to it by the Constitution that we are closer to being serfs than citizens and closer to being "citizens of the world" than citizens of our respective states!

A Conspiracy

That's unconstitutional, illegal, crosswise of the law of the land, and a damned conspiracy. Then these schemers have the nerve to call those of us who expose them "conspiracy theorists." No, we're "conspiracy revealers."

Don't Blame Guns

I am sympathetic with those who have lost children or other loved ones at the hands of killers. However, the gun didn't decide to kill anyone, the killer did. Australia has gone so far as to ban rocks as lethal weapons if carried by certain people in protests or in cases of aggravated assault. Rocks? Yes, anything can be used by one individual to kill another. There were thousands of years of killing before the invention of guns.

The right of the individual to have a gun is not to be infringed. That means, in our vernacular, that government has

Unconstitutional Theories "Justifying" Federal Gun Control

Much of [the twentieth century] has been a time when the federal government has ignored the limitations imposed on it by the Constitution. Recent cases decided by the Supreme Court indicate that the Justices are beginning to once again take the Constitution and their oath of office seriously. As Justice Clarence Thomas put it in the recent *Lopez* case, "our case law has drifted far from the original understanding . . ." of the Constitution.

While there were wrong turns before this century, much of the unconstitutional rule from Washington dates back to the Great Depression and its war on crime and war on the bank crisis. There were many unconstitutional theories of government pursued to justify the power grab by Washington. One of the theories was to run an end run around constitutional limitations by entering into a treaty that would require passage of legislation accomplishing what, without the treaty, would have been unconstitutional.

President Franklin Delano Roosevelt's administration was an active participant in the Disarmament Conference of 1934. Roosevelt sought Senate ratification of an Arms Traffic Convention but was unsuccessful. Had the treaty been ratified, Roosevelt would have obtained the alleged authority to have Congress infringe on the right to keep and bear arms pursuant to the treaty powers of Article VI, paragraph 2.

Roosevelt then shifted to the unconstitutional, non-existent doctrine of emergency powers to justify enactment of gun control at the federal level. Calling for a War on Crime and Gangsters, Roosevelt persuaded Congress to pass a series of bills federalizing various crimes and compelling the registration of machine guns and sawed-off shotguns and rifles. The formula "War on Whatever" became a decades long federal government weapon for usurping powers not delegated to it.

Nowhere does the Constitution give the President or the Congress the power to federalize state crimes or enact gun control legislation—not even in a national emergency.

Larry Pratt, "Unconstitutional Theories 'Justifying' Federal Gun Control," Gunowners.org, March 1995. www.gunowners.org.

---

no business sticking its nose into our possession or non-possession of guns. Period. All governments that want to oppress the citizenry grab their guns. How about "gun registration?" Well that's infringement. Do you expect a Mafia or other gang member to line up and state their purpose for having one or more guns is to commit crimes? No. That's idiotic. Only law-abiding citizens will put up with gun registration, and it's about time the citizens realized that what they are doing is abiding by unconstitutional laws that infringe on their rights. That is the road to totalitarianism.

And then there's the wimpy excuse "well, I'm not afraid to register my gun, I don't commit crimes." Of course not. No criminal registers his guns any more than he fills out an application to commit a crime. Good grief, use some damned common sense, folks, and figure out what "gun control" is all about. The problem in this nation is that the citizens take freedom for granted, and that is precisely why we have so little of it left to us. Younger folks have no ability to remember when we had a free country, people my age and older recall a much freer one, and my grandparents recalled a much freer nation yet. They were pioneers in the Arizona Territory!

The use of technology to better the quality of life does not demand surrender of an equal amount of freedom, which is precisely the non-equation the government is trying to patch together. That's about as idiotic as trying to explain the theory of relativity to Einstein, or how a light bulb works to Edison.

Natural Law

There is something in the way of "natural law" that can be awkwardly stated this way: "When the government begins to fear the people, it invents good reasons to persuade the citizens that serfdom offers safety and security when the true objective is enslavement to the rulers." Please do not quote me on that, work it into a better natural law and enunciate it in clearer and more concise terms. It is immaterial who is credited with the words, the objective is to wake the people out of stupor and call on them to stop surrendering to the forces of evil power that have taken away the very freedom they are taking for granted. I know people who actually believe our gold reserves are in Ft. Knox and that we're still on a hard currency standard. Incredible? Those same people have told me that we need to give up some of our freedoms for safety.

Yes, it is a temptation to slap the crap out of them. Free people do not worry about safety and security, they are concerned with liberty. That statement sank Barry Goldwater's presidential candidacy, people in 1964 had already become the sucklings of the nanny state and feared a return to personal responsibility.

Guns are instruments, neutral, they do not go on shooting rampages. People do. They use the guns for wrong purposes. The same is true of irresponsible drivers, corrupt officials, and drug dealers. Drugs don't wander around looking for someone to sniff them or smoke them or inject them. People sell drugs to people willing to do these things. The blame is always, always, always and forever on the people, not the objects they use. Get that straight, please. Any other thinking is blame—shoving or responsibility—dodging.

Our Duty as Americans

People who fear God have little to fear from anything or anyone else. People who do not fear God have good reason to fear just about everything, principally death.

However we all have a duty, implied by the Bill of Rights, to keep ourselves, our families and our nation free from oppressors. It is the well-armed militias that will get that job done, organized or not.

Any infringement of our right to keep and bear arms is a threat to our entire freedom. This nation was born in revolution, and the leaders fear another one by the people who object to more severe oppression than old King George III ever dreamed of imposing.

Save the tea, throw the corrupt leaders into Boston Harbor.

Keep your guns, ammo and rights free from criminals, especially those in public office.

Periodical Bibliography

The following articles have been selected to supplement the diverse views presented in this chapter.

Jeff Cohen	"Gun Control, the NRA, and the Second Amendment," *FAIR*, February 2000. www.fair.org.
Amitai Etzioni	"Reasonable Regulation," *National Law Journal*, April 5, 2004.
Stephen Halbrook	"Deconstructing the Second Amendment," *NewsMax.com*, November 3, 2000. www.newsmax.com.
James B. Jacobs	"'Right to Bear Arms' Decision Would Improve Gun Control," *USA Today*, December 15, 2002.
Dave Kopel	"Arms Alive," *National Review Online*, November 3, 2004. www.nationalreview.com.
Dave Kopel	"Explaining Eisentrager," *National Review Online*, April 20, 2004. www.nationalreview.com.
Dave Kopel	"The Second Amendment Before the Court," *Liberty*, December 2003.
Dahlia Lithwick	"What Does the Second Amendment Say About the Right to Own Guns?" *Slate*, July 10, 2001. www.slate.com.
Nelson Lund	"Taking the Second Amendment Seriously," *Weekly Standard*, July 24, 2000.
Mary McGrory	"Lock and Load Ashcroft," *Washington Post*, May 19, 2002.
Richard Poe	"Who Will Speak for the Second Amendment?" *FrontPageMag.com*, July 4, 2001. www.frontpagemag.com.
Eugene Volokh	"Who's Right on Second," *National Review Online*, December 6, 2002. www.nationalreview.com.

CHAPTER 4

How Can Gun Violence Be Reduced?

Chapter Preface

As the gun control debate has continued into the twenty-first century, commentators still disagree on the best way to reduce gun violence. Gun control advocates favor stronger gun control legislation; gun rights activists vehemently oppose any restrictions on gun ownership. In recent years new technologies have emerged that have impacted the gun control debate, giving rise to new controversies. One such technology is the trigger lock, which is installed on a firearm and requires the owner to know the proper combination in order to fire the gun. Another technology is the smart gun, which only fires when it recognizes the gun owner's thumbprint.

Trigger locks are devices designed to prevent guns from going off accidentally. Ranging from keyed devices to combination locks and alarms, trigger locks are viewed by gun control advocates as an inexpensive way to ensure that unsupervised children will not accidentally fire a gun kept in the home. These analysts contend that trigger locks reduce the number of unintentional firearm deaths and suicides. Recent studies have shown that nearly 75 percent of Americans think that trigger locks should be required for all handguns. However, opponents of the trigger lock claim that the mechanisms vary greatly in quality; in some cases, children have been able to break or bypass the device, they claim. Also, these commentators argue, a trigger lock will increase the time it takes for a gun owner to act in self-defense.

Smart guns, also known as personalized guns, are firearms designed to be fired only by the gun's owner. Smart guns recognize the registered owner's thumbprint and will not fire for anyone else. Gun manufacturers are still developing and testing the technology, but proponents expect that the smart gun will reduce unintentional firearm suicides and deaths. Smart guns, they argue, can also reduce the gun violence that results from stolen guns, and are more effective than trigger locks and other removable devices. On the other hand, opponents say that the high cost of such personalized weapons will prohibit poor families from obtaining guns for protection. These analysts also assert that smart gun technology is still in its infancy and will not be of practical use for some time to come, if it ever is.

Americans are overwhelmingly in favor of technology that will reduce accidental deaths and suicides without inhibiting gun owners' ability to defend themselves from criminals. These technologies illustrate the public's desire to minimize the harms associated with firearms while maximizing the possible benefits. The authors in the following chapter debate other approaches to reducing gun violence. As these arguments show, reducing firearm deaths and injuries often involves an infringement on the public's access to guns, a trade-off that remains highly controversial.

VIEWPOINT

1

"There are scores of reasonable policies that could reduce U.S. firearm injuries while keeping almost all of the recreational and self-defense benefits of firearms."

America Needs Stronger Gun Control Laws

David Hemenway

In the following viewpoint David Hemenway offers several policy proposals that he claims will work to reduce gun violence in the United States. These include safe gun storage practices, government regulation of firearms as a consumer product, a national gun registration, and a government group that investigates every incident of gun violence. A former Pew Fellow on Injury Control, Hemenway is a professor of health policy at the Harvard School of Public Health and director of Harvard's Injury Control Research Center and Youth Violence Prevention Center.

As you read, consider the following questions:

1. How can Hollywood help to reduce gun violence, in Hemenway's view?
2. According to the author, what can gun manufacturers do to reduce gun violence?
3. How can police and community activities curtail gun violence, in the author's opinion?

David Hemenway, *Private Guns, Public Health*. Ann Arbor: University of Michigan Press. Copyright © 2004 by the University of Michigan. All rights reserved. Reproduced by permission.

However they are categorized, there are scores of reasonable policies that could reduce U.S. firearm injuries while keeping almost all of the recreational and self-defense benefits of firearms. . . . This [viewpoint] highlights those policies that may reduce our firearms problem and are acceptable to the large majority of Americans. This approach is consistent with the underlying assumptions of the 1994 Task Force on Gun Violence of the American Bar Association (ABA):

> While the ABA has steadfastly recognized the traditions of gun ownership for sporting purposes and for self-defense, there is nothing inconsistent with those traditions in requiring guns to carry safety features to protect children, or in requiring firearms dealers to operate bona fide businesses, or in requiring licenses and education of handgun owners. Personal responsibility and accountability for safety and protection of others must be required of every firearms dealer, every hunter and every parent who maintains a firearm in their home. (American Bar Association Task Force 1994)

Those Who Can Play a Role

At the nongovernmental level, schools, community organizations, medical professionals, the media, private companies, and others can play an important role in reducing firearm violence. Education is needed, perhaps through local parent-teacher associations, particularly concerning children and guns. Two pressing topics are gun storage practices and teaching parents routinely to inquire about possible access to firearms when their children are invited to friends' houses.

Medical professionals can influence their patients to improve their gun safety I.Q. In one study, almost three-quarters of gun-owning parents said they were very likely to follow a pediatrician's recommendations regarding the safe storage of firearms.

Hollywood can also do its part by modeling nonviolent nongun behavior and safe gun practices. Television shows helped spread the idea of a designated driver and have promoted seat belt use by having the shows' role models buckle up. With this in mind, public health injury-control experts have been meeting with members of Hollywood's creative community to explore ways the medium can promote safe and responsible gun ownership and use.

Private companies that ship firearms need to be more vigilant. Gun thefts sometimes rely on someone working inside a packaging center. In 1999, United Parcel Service changed its gun shipping policy to reduce theft. All gun shipments must now be sent by overnight airmail rather than by ground transportation. This policy reduces transit time and the number of people who handle the package, thus reducing the likelihood of theft (Wolcott 1999).

A New, Gun-Regulating Government Agency

In terms of governmental policy, a crucial first step is to create a new agency or provide an existing agency with the power to regulate firearms as a consumer product. The agency should create and maintain a national violent death data system (a surveillance system) that provides information on the circumstances and weapon for every fatality, along with a sample of nonfatal firearm injuries. The agency should make that information readily available and provide funds for social scientists, criminologists, and other expert researchers interested in reducing firearm violence and firearm injuries. For the first time, comprehensive data would be available to guide and evaluate firearm policy.

The agency should also investigate in-depth a sample of gun injuries. When an airplane crashes, the National Transportation Safety Board investigates what went wrong so that future tragedies can be prevented. By contrast, when a gun tragedy occurs, little is done to explore what happened and thereby prevent the next catastrophe. This needs to be changed. For a sample of firearm injuries, a team of behavioral, engineering, and policy experts should systematically investigate the facts and circumstances surrounding the incidents and recommend changes that could prevent future firearm injuries.

The agency should have the power to require safety and crime-fighting characteristics on all firearms manufactured or sold in the United States. For example, guns should not fire when dropped and should be made childproof (a toddler should not be able to fire any gun). Pistols should have magazine safeties that prevent firing once the clip has been removed. The agency should have the power to ensure that every gun has a unique identifier, that the serial number is virtually impossible to obliterate, and that bullets can be readily traced to a particular gun. The agency should have the funds to promote research on personalized or "smart guns" and on less lethal ammunition and weapons.

Thompson. © by Copley News Service. Reproduced by permission.

The agency should have the power to ban from regular civilian use certain products that are not needed for protection and endanger the public. As bazookas, machine guns, and plastic guns have been banned, so probably should caseless ammunition and .50-caliber bullets. Except perhaps for bona fide collectors, the agency should prohibit the manufacture, possession, and sale of silencers, short-barreled shotguns, large capacity ammunition magazines, and "gadget" guns that are difficult for metal detectors to identify or are disguised as innocuous items such as key chains, cigarette lighters, or pens. The agency should also have jurisdiction over firearm-related products, such as laser sights, trigger activators, and ammunition. The agency should also have the power to prevent the introduction into the civilian market of new firearm products that are more lethal, more concealable, or more conducive to crime than current firearms. The key point is not to prescribe exactly what the agency would or should do but to create such an agency and invest it with the resources and power—including standard setting, recall, and research capability—for making reasonable decisions about firearms. The power to determine the side-impact performance standards for automobiles resides with a regulatory agency, as does the power to decide whether or not to ban three-wheeled all-terrain vehicles (while allowing the safer four-wheeled models). Similarly, each specific rule regulating the firearm as a product should go through an administrative rather than a legislative process.

Gun Control Laws

To reduce criminal gun use, all gun sales and other nonfamily transfers should be required to go through licensed dealers. In addition, the dealers should make such sales only from their licensed retail premises—not from their home kitchens, garages, or automobile trunks. These simple requirements will help eliminate the enormous secondary-market loophole that currently makes it ridiculously easy for juveniles, criminals, and terrorists to obtain firearms at flea markets and gun shows and through friends.

Licensed dealers should be under greater scrutiny from both the manufacturers and the government. The Bureau of Alcohol, Tobacco, and Firearms should have the ability to bring felony suits against rogue dealers and make unannounced visits at the bureau's discretion. Background checks should be required for all gun store employees. All firearm thefts should be reported.

To reduce gunrunning, there should be a national law prohibiting the sale of more than one handgun per month to any single individual. Police should routinely trace all crime guns, as is done in drug enforcement, to help identify and prosecute illegal sellers.

At the level of the individual gun user, gun possession should be banned for those convicted of violent crimes—misdemeanors as well as felonies. A national waiting period for gun purchases should be reenacted to reduce homicides and suicides resulting from momentary impulses. The legal age for gun ownership should be raised: just as the national minimum legal drinking age is twenty-one, so too should the legal age for possessing a handgun be twenty-one (although a lower age for long guns is probably reasonable).

To reduce criminal access to firearms, there should be licensing of gun owners and registration of guns. Licensing and registration are currently required of automobile owners and do not limit the availability of motor vehicles. Licensing and registration of guns are policies used by most other high-income countries as part of their overall regulation of firearms. Some twenty U.S. states already have licensing and/or registration requirements.

Laws Regarding the Sale of Firearms

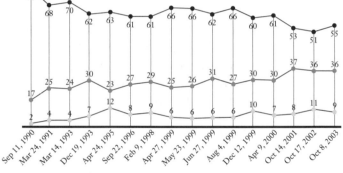

"Laws Regarding Sale of Firearms, 2003," The Gallup Organization, 2004.

A licensing system will reduce gunrunning from states with lax gun controls to states with stringent gun controls. A national handgun license card will make it more difficult for gunrunners to obtain fake identification documents and tougher for violent persons to use temporary residences in other states to buy guns they could not purchase in their home states. To obtain a handgun license, the individual should pass a fingerprint-based background check and complete an approved handgun safety course.

Registration of guns will allow all legal firearm transfers to be tracked. Current gun tracing typically provides information only about the initial retail sale. A registration system will make it difficult for an individual to act as a straw purchaser (someone with a clean record who buys guns for a criminal). Registration records will make it possible to identify straw buyers, gunrunners, and rogue dealers.

Guns Entail Responsibility

Gun ownership, possession, and carrying entail responsibilities. To prevent theft, accidents, and suicide, some countries require that guns be stored unloaded and locked, with the ammunition kept separately. Just as swimming pool owners are liable for misadventures if they do not reasonably restrict access, so should gun owners be held liable for juvenile misuse when guns are stored inappropriately. Some scholars argue for strict liability for gun owners to encourage safe storage and other responsible behaviors. Others suggest that just as liability insurance is typically mandated for automobile owners, gun owners might also be required to purchase liability coverage for injuries caused by their firearms.

Drinking is legal and driving is legal, but we have wisely made it illegal to drink and drive, even if the driver has not broken any other law. Similarly we should make the combination of heavy drinking and gun carrying illegal. Gun-carrying laws should give police discretion to prohibit gun carrying by persons they believe to be dangerous to the community.

Because of the external costs imposed on society by gun availability, the tax on the retail sales of guns and ammunition should be increased. The revenue should be earmarked to help underwrite the direct costs of gun injuries (e.g., medical care) and gun-related regulatory activities (e.g., surveillance, licensing).

Many creative police tactics and community activities should be used to reduce gun violence. A [1999] U.S. Department of Justice publication describes sixty different "promising strategies"—innovative local programs designed to reduce gun violence. For example, in 1994, Rhode Island established the nation's first stand-alone Gun Court to increase the speed of disposition and level and certainty of punishment. In Detroit, a court-based intervention program requires gun violence education for gun-toting youths as a condition of their bond.

In some communities, police have created special teams that target illegal gun traffickers (Charleston, West Virginia), scofflaw dealers (Oakland, California), and violent career criminals (Charlotte, North Carolina). Memphis has created a Weapon Watch hotline that allows students anonymously to report fellow students who bring firearms to school. In Baton Rouge, police-probation teams implement intensive, regular home visits to monitor probation compliance. Various other campaigns are designed to promote safe gun storage, change truant youths' attitudes about guns and violence, and prevent at-risk youths from becoming involved with gangs.

Many other policies merit attention. Voluntary gun buyback programs for example, have a minimal effect on street gun violence but could reduce gun accidents, suicides, and the use of firearms in domestic disputes. Firearm advertising probably should be monitored more closely; for example, in the 1990s, many ads deceptively implied that handguns in the homes were preventive for children, wives, and family members in general. This list is not comprehensive. It merely indicates some of the many policies that, when combined, can effectively decrease firearm crime and injuries.

"Study after study shows that increasing gun control laws leads to an increase in crime rather than a decline."

America Does Not Need Stronger Gun Control Laws

Steve Pudlo

In the following viewpoint Steve Pudlo contends that the more gun control laws that are passed, the more violent gun crime there is in the United States. Instead of passing more laws, America needs more firearms in the hands of citizens, he argues. According to Pudlo, if criminals know their potential victims will be armed, they will get out of the crime business. Pudlo teaches computer applications at Three Rivers Community College and Eastern Connecticut State University.

As you read, consider the following questions:

1. What is the symbiotic relationship between guns and criminals, in Pudlo's opinion?
2. According to the author, why do gun control advocates lobby for more gun control legislation when studies show that more gun control laws results in more gun violence?
3. According to Pudlo, what is the best defense against criminals?

Let's talk a bit about symbiotic relationships. A symbiotic relationship is a relationship whereby each partner gains from the contributions of the other. The partners feed off each other in an orgy of mutual parasitism, and in the symbiology, each partner gains more than they lose. The benefits outweigh the costs.

Unorthodox Symbiosis

An example of an unorthodox symbiosis is the way that the insurance industry benefits from burglary. (Huh?) how is that possible? Well, let us think of it this way: What if there were no burglaries at all. None. Nobody burgled anybody else, no one stole from another, no one took what didn't belong to them. Ideal world? Perhaps, but if no one stole, why buy insurance? Why patronize a business guarding against what doesn't happen? Indeed. Now you are beginning to understand the concept of a symbiotic relationship between antagonists. Neither side is overtly cooperating with the other, yet they need each other. If there were no burglaries, there would be no need for burglary insurance. If there were no burglary insurance, the consequences of burglary would increase to the point where they would drive the burglars out of the burglary business, then there would be no need for burglary insurance . . . and the cycle goes on. So the insurance industry needs for the crime of burglary to exist, for their own existence, but only to the level of where the crimes hurt the insurance company's ability to pay claims.

Another example of a symbiotic relationship between antagonists is the relationship between armed criminals and the gun control industry. If there were no crimes involving guns, there would be no need for gun control. If there were no gun control, then (theoretically) crime would rise to the point where gun control would be needed to curb crime.

If the symbiosis exists that would be the situation. In practice, things break down, illustrating that the control of guns is tangentially (if ever) related to the suppression of crime. Study after study shows that increasing gun control laws leads to an increase in crime rather than a decline. If you look at Washington, DC, you see a prime example of this paradigm on a statewide scale, and you can look at England,

Canada and/or Australia to see this happen on a countrywide scale. Has there ever been an example of gun control resulting in a lowering of crime? If so, I am not aware of it. Yet why does high crime inspire more and more solutions of more and more gun control?

A Symbiotic Relationship

Perhaps less crime is not the objective. Perhaps there does exist a symbiotic relationship between crime and some sort of control? Perhaps some folks are using high crime and gun control as tools in a bid to exert more control over the population? When you look at the calculus of gun control versus crime, the numbers don't add up. It's a losing proposition. Gun control causes crime to rise. Period. The statistics show this as an undeniable fact, yet cries for more gun control continue. Why? And what lies behind this?

You take away an individual's ability (and thereby right) to defend himself against hostility by a criminal, and you also take away his ability (and right) to resist authority (government). By taking that ability away, you embolden the criminal, lower his occupational risks, lower the cost of getting into the business, and you open the field of criminality to more participants. If you make it easier, less costly, to become a doctor, then more people can and will become doctors. If you make it easier, less risky, to become a criminal, then more people will become criminals. More criminals require more victims to support them, which means more crime. More crime results in the government calling for more gun control, which takes away more people's ability to defend themselves, which lowers the risks and costs of becoming a criminal, and you have not a symbiotic relationship, but a vicious cycle. But to what end?

Other band-aid solutions to high crime are what? More police. More laws. More cost to the taxpayer rendering him more subservient and dependent upon the government for his daily subsistence. People who used to be able to rely upon themselves for protection against relatively few criminals, now mostly rely upon a more bloated, expensive and ineffective government to protect them from more criminals. The net result is that the criminal class booms, and the middle class pays more and more for less and less protection.

The real solution to high crime is for the government to put up real deterrence to the criminal—increase his costs of doing business to the point where he chooses another occupation. If fewer people become criminals, there would be less crime, and everybody would benefit. So a method of pricing criminals out of business is needed in order to deal with the issue. . . .

Get Criminals Out of the Crime Business

There are two ways to do this. One way is to increase the penalties for getting caught. Whilst this is a relatively expensive prospect to the criminal, the key concept is that in order for this to occur, the government needs to catch the criminal. Few criminals believe that they will ever be caught, or else they wouldn't be criminals. So the calculus of being caught wouldn't normally enter the thought process of anybody contemplating a crime. Therefore, the concept of affecting a change in behavior relative to getting caught, amongst folks who don't think that they will be caught, is of dubious real value.

The second manner is to increase the occupational risk factors for the criminals beyond their acceptable threshold. If the risk of being injured or killed is significant, then one would have to be insane to continue down that career path, correct? Of course the criminal would have to be aware of this. Well, if the risk of being resisted, and perhaps injured/killed was raised, then it would stand to reason that fewer people would be attracted to the field. With fewer practitioners, there would logically be fewer crimes, crime would go down, and so would public outcry for a solution as crime becomes less a worry. The easiest method of accomplishing this would be to simply allow the people the ability to defend themselves.

If a criminal fears that the person he is about to accost can and will resist, he is more likely to take care, or even choose another target. If he perceives that any target has an equal likelihood to oppose, resist or even damage him, then he would be far more likely to abandon that method of livelihood. Is this a good thing?

The Case Against Gun Control

Few public policy debates have been as dominated by emotion and misinformation as the one on gun control. Perhaps this debate is so highly charged because it involves such fundamental issues. The calls for more gun restrictions or for bans on some or all guns are calls for significant change in our social and constitutional systems.

Gun control is based on the faulty notion that ordinary American citizens are too clumsy and ill-tempered to be trusted with weapons. Only through the blatant abrogation of explicit constitutional rights is gun control even possible. It must be enforced with such violations of individual rights as intrusive search and seizure. It most severely victimizes those who most need weapons for self-defense, such as blacks and women.

The various gun control proposals on today's agenda—including licensing, waiting periods, and bans on so-called Saturday night specials—are of little, if any, value as crime-fighting measures. Banning guns to reduce crime makes as much sense as banning alcohol to reduce drunk driving. Indeed, persuasive evidence shows that civilian gun ownership can be a powerful deterrent to crime.

The gun control debate poses the basic question: Who is more trustworthy, the government or the people?

Dave B. Kopel, "Trust the People: The Case Against Gun Control," Cato Institute, July 11, 1998.

Well, the most effective means of doing just this is to allow people to arm themselves with firearms. Note that I specified firearms. Projectile weapons. Guns. Means to kill. Effective self defense weapons. Think about it. If someone approaches you armed with a weapon, what is the safest and most effective method of repelling the attack? Should one run? What if the criminal gives chase, or shoots at you? Usually running is not a viable option. And while talking to the criminal has been known to dissuade an attack, that event is far more the exception than the rule—more often arguing will only enrage the criminal. Screaming, sirens, and whistles can provide an audience, and even that is not guaranteed. Brandishing a knife or other close quarters weapon has a better likelihood of being taken as a challenge than a threat. Imagine someone who makes their living by violence feeling threatened by someone with little or no experience using a weapon!

Some of the newer technologies are of dubious value—they either require too much distance from the criminal, or too little. Some of them take several seconds to take effect, giving the criminal time to retaliate by shooting, slashing, or using other methods to overcome your resistance. Even if he does go down, it isn't really successful if he gets the opportunity to take you down with him, is it?

A Successful Defense

That leaves us with firearms. Range isn't terribly important, you can shoot a criminal from close or far (too far and the criminal isn't a danger). You can stop him immediately, and since the fact that you have a gun means that you can inflict harm on the criminal before he can inflict harm on you, you suddenly have the upper hand, and the criminal is faced with reevaluating his career choice. If he's lucky, he'll merely be arrested, if not he's not going to need asbestos underwear.

In either event, a successful defense against a criminal has a ripple effect amongst society. Criminals get to understand that crime isn't as easy and profitable as it might have once been, more criminals are on hiatus in the jail or morgue, and finally, people feel safer. People feel safer, people feel more empowered to take responsibility for their own lives, become more independent. Society loses criminals and gains productive workers without having to afford the enormous costs of huge prison complexes. The government has no excuse to increase control over its subjects.

Or maybe that's the real reason why things are the way they remain. Symbiosis, remember?

"Ideally, all retail gun sales should be regulated to protect the public from unreasonable risk of injury and death."

Laws Regulating Gun Show Sales Should Be Tightened

Consumer Federation of America

Under current federal law only Federal Firearms License holders are required to conduct purchaser background checks when conducting a sale at gun shows. Unlicensed holders, such as individuals wishing to sell family-owned firearms, are not required to do these checks. In the following viewpoint the Consumer Federation of America (CFA) contends that this loophole must be closed in order to prevent criminals—who could not purchase firearms legally from licensed dealers—from buying guns from nonlicensed individuals at gun shows. The CFA is an advocacy, research, and service organization working on behalf of consumers.

As you read, consider the following questions:

1. Under current law, who is allowed to buy guns from unlicensed dealers at gun shows?
2. What five principles must be upheld when crafting legislation to close the gun show loophole, in the author's opinion?
3. Do Americans support closing the gun show loophole, according to recent polls?

Consumer Federation of America "Don't Just Close the Gun-Show Loophole—Close It Effectively," www.consumerfed.org, 2005.

The gun show loophole allows felons, domestic abusers, minors, and other prohibited persons to purchase guns without background checks.

The Loophole

How does this happen? Current federal law only requires Federal Firearms License (FFLs) holders to conduct Brady background checks on gun show sales. The loophole is that unlicensed private individuals are not required to conduct the Brady checks. So, convicted felons and other prohibited persons buy guns at gun shows from these unlicensed private individuals to avoid background checks.

The public supports closing this deadly loophole. The 1999 National Gun Policy Survey, conducted by the National Opinion Research Center, found that nearly eight out of 10 Americans (79 percent) would favor a law that required private gun sales to be subject to the same background check requirements as sales by licensed dealers. This belief is shared by America's gun owners. Two-thirds of Americans who personally own a gun would favor such a law.

Consumer Federation of America (CFA) wants to see the gun industry regulated for health and safety like virtually every other industry, and closing the gun show loophole is an important step in that direction. Ideally, all retail gun sales should be regulated to protect the public from unreasonable risk of injury and death.

How the Loophole Can Be Closed

In order to close the gun show loophole effectively, the following five principles must be upheld:

1. *Legislation to close the gun show loophole should build on the Brady Law not weaken it.* Under the existing National Instant Criminal Background Check System (NICS)—the system which implements the background check required under the 1993 Brady Handgun Violence Prevention Act—three business days are allowed to complete suspicious checks. The NRA [National Rifle Association] argues that the 3-business days allowed to complete the checks holds up legitimate gun buyers. That's not true. According to the Department of Justice, *95 percent of all checks are completed within two hours,* and

22 percent of all gun buyers who are found to be prohibited persons are not found to be prohibited until more than 72 hours have passed. Ultimately, the NRA wants Congress to reduce the three business day period to 24 hours. This would not be effective because it would establish lesser requirements for gun shows than those which currently apply to sales at gun stores. It would have the negative effect of drawing more criminals to gun shows since they would have a better chance of slipping through the cracks. It may sell more guns, but it would put the public at risk.

Components of the National Firearm Check System

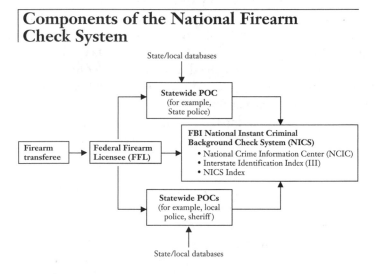

Michael Bowling et al., *Background Checks for Firearm Transfers, 2002*, Bureau of Justice Statistics, U.S. Department of Justice, Washington, DC, September 2003.

2. *The integrity of the National Instant Criminal Background Check System (NICS) must not be undermined.* The Justice Department currently allows records generated by the NICS to be kept for 90 days for audit purposes. The FBI needs this period to insure that the system is functioning properly. The NRA supports efforts to immediately destroy essential records maintained under NICS. This would weaken efforts to ensure the Brady bill's effectiveness.

3. *Access to the NICS system should not be expanded.* During debate last Congress [2003], NRA-sponsored amendments

[which did not pass] would have created a new class of licensee, who would be granted access to the NICS to facilitate non-dealer sales. In 1999 Senator and NRA Board Member Larry Craig (R-ID) offered an NRA-drafted amendment that would have created a new classification of licensees called "special registrants" with access to the NICS in order to perform background checks at gun shows. Representative John Conyers (D-MI), ranking Democrat on the House Judiciary Committee, expressed his concern that "the creation of a new entity entrusted with conducting accurate background checks and safeguarding the privacy of the system is an invitation to organized crime front operations' fraudulently conducting background checks and misusing the system." Furthermore, the creation of a network of special registrants could severely tax the resources available to the Bureau of Alcohol, Tobacco, and Firearms (BATF) to conduct routine inspections and ensure compliance with applicable laws.

Another potential danger posed by "special registrants" is that they could easily become a new class of gun *seller.* The NRA has made reversing the decrease in the number of FFLs a high-priority issue. In its latest issue of *America's 1st Freedom* NRA Executive Vice President Wayne LaPierre addressed the issue in his column, proclaiming, "BATF's blatant anti-dealer policies—which have harassed thousands out of business—must be reversed." The NRA clearly wants to increase the number of gun sellers, which would ultimately allow criminals easier access to guns.

4. *Gun show legislation must ensure that all guns sold at such shows can be efficiently traced if they turn up in a crime scene.* For example, three of the guns used in the Columbine High School shooting which were purchased at a gun show were not easily traceable because they had been sold through private sellers without background checks and the required recordkeeping. The goal of effective crime gun tracing would be undermined by the creation of a new category of licensees with fewer recordkeeping duties than full fledged FFLs. Scrupulous recordkeeping is essential to the effectiveness of gun show legislation.

5. *Regulations must be applied to all guns shows.* In order to be effective, the legislation must apply to all events at which

guns are sold in any volume, such as gun shows, flea markets, or swap meets. It is imperative that the definition of gun show ensure that transactions initiated at a gun show cannot be consummated off-premises with no background check required. Effective legislation should mandate a background check if any part of a firearm transaction (including the offer for sale, transfer, or exchange) takes place at a gun show. Criminals are sure to exploit a "let's step outside" loophole that would allow unscrupulous gun sellers to use gun shows as venues for arranging sales and then finalizing them off-site to avoid background checks.

There is general agreement about the need to close the gun show loophole. However, closing the current gun show loophole by creating new and bigger loopholes in federal law will not protect the public. Congress must assure that all of the above issues are addressed in crafting an effective solution.

4

"Rather than expanding the flawed NICS to cover the small number of private sales at gun shows, money could be better spent . . . prosecuting the felons who have already purchased guns illegally."

Laws Regulating Gun Show Sales Should Not Be Tightened

H. Sterling Burnett

In the following viewpoint, excerpted from testimony given before the Louisiana House of Representatives in opposition to H.B. 245, a proposed law that would allow only licensed dealers to sell guns at gun shows, H. Sterling Burnett asserts that gun control advocates are working to close a nonexistent loophole. In his view most gun dealers at gun shows are licensed and perform the required checks. Furthermore, he argues that the number of unlicensed dealers is far less than has been reported. Private transactions between individuals, he asserts, should not be subject to the same regulations as a licensed dealer who makes multiple sales would be. The law did not pass. Burnett is a senior fellow for the National Center for Policy Analysis (NCPA). He specializes in issues involving environmental and gun policy.

As you read, consider the following questions:
1. How does the National Instant Check System (NICS) work?
2. According to the author, why is there no need to enlarge NICS to cover gun shows?
3. How effective is NICS in preventing criminals from buying guns?

H. Sterling Burnett, testimony before the Louisiana House Committee on Administration of Criminal Justice, Baton Rouge, LA, April 28, 2004.

One recurrent *bete noir* of gun control activists is the so-called gun show loophole. Gun control proponents have claimed that up to 70 percent of guns used in crimes come from gun shows. Handgun Control, Inc. (HCI) says "25–50 percent of the vendors at most gun shows are unlicensed dealers." Thus, they argue, conducting background checks on all buyers at gun shows—whether they purchase from licensed or "unlicensed dealers"—will deny children and criminals access to firearms.

This argument has some appeal to those seeking an easy fix to mass public shootings. But their arguments are wrong—mandating background checks at gun shows will not reduce crime significantly. Indeed, their proposed solutions could make crime problems worse. Rather than closing a loophole in current law, mandatory checks will be a step towards banning private firearms sales between individuals.

The National Instant Check System

The National Instant Check System (NICS) took effect November 30, 1998, creating "a national database containing records of persons who are disqualified from receiving firearms." Under NICS, dealers must clear every firearms purchase through a background check of the prospective buyer by the FBI. The dealer calls NICS and provides an operator with: (1) his Federal firearms license number and unique password; (2) the potential buyer's name, date of birth, sex and race; (3) and the type of gun to be transferred, handgun or long gun.

The operator checks the data against NICS's database of prohibited persons and either approves or delays the sale. A delay indicates that the check turned up information that requires further review by an analyst, who by law has up to three business days to approve or deny the sale—longer than the duration of most gun shows, which last over a weekend.

A mid-1980s National Institute of Justice (NIJ) study of convicted felons in 12 state prisons found that criminals purchased firearms at gun shows so rarely that those purchases were not worth reporting as a separate category.

The evidence indicates that criminal demand for firearms did not shift to gun shows after the 1994 Brady Law mandated background checks for all gun purchases from licensed dealers. The most recent federal report on the matter, a November 2001 Bureau of Justice Statistics (BJS) report, *Firearm Use by Offenders*, found that only 0.7 percent of state inmates possessing firearms got them from gun shows—fewer than got them at flea markets (1.0 percent). Earlier studies confirm these results. For instance:

- A June 2000, BJS report, *Federal Firearm Offenders, 1992–98*, found that just 8 of the 288 defendants (2.8 percent) convicted in U.S. District Courts for illegal receipt or transfer of a firearm got their weapons from currently legal, non-retail transactions at gun shows.
- An NIJ study released in December 1997 said only 2 percent of criminal guns came from gun shows.
- A study of youthful offenders in Michigan, presented at a meeting of the American Society of Criminology, found that only 3 percent had acquired their last handgun at a gun show—and many of the purchases were made by "straw purchasers" (i.e., legal gun buyers illegally acting as surrogates for criminals).
- A 1997 report by the U.S. Bureau of Justice Statistics on federal firearms offenders said only 1.7 percent of crime guns are acquired at gun shows.
- According to a report issued by the educational arm of Handgun Control, only two of 48 major city police chiefs said that gun show sales were an important problem in their city.

The claim that a quarter to half of the vendors at most gun shows are unlicensed dealers is true only if one counts vendors selling items other than guns (e.g., books, clothing, ammunition, knives, holsters and other accessories) as unlicensed dealers.

The Federal Firearms License

Federal law requires that any person "engaged in the business" of selling firearms possess a valid Federal Firearms License. This is true whether one is selling guns for a living at a gun store or at a gun show. Licensed dealers must conduct an NICS check prior to the transfer of any firearm—regardless of where that transfer occurs. The majority of sellers of firearms at gun shows are licensed dealers and do conduct checks.

Individuals who occasionally sell or trade guns from their personal collection need not be licensed nor are they required to conduct a NICS check prior to the sale—whether the sale occurs at a gun show, at their home or out of the trunk of their car. Congress never intended a person who wants to sell a spare hunting rifle to a friend, a father who wishes to give a .22 rifle to his son or a widow who wishes to dispose of her late husband's firearms through an Internet auction or an ad in the local paper to undertake a NICS background check.

Thus, the same laws apply to gun shows as to all other gun transactions—there is no loophole.

NICS Failures

A General Accounting Office report, "Gun Control: Implementation of NICS," was issued on February 29, 2000. It documents many NICS failures. With a congressional allocation of more than $300 million since 1995:

- Through September 1999, NICS had 360 unscheduled outages amounting to more than 215 hours of downtime, during which firearms retailers suffered millions of dollars in lost sales.
- The system failed to provide instant checks 28 percent of the time, delaying sales for 1.2 million legal purchasers from hours to days.
- Of the 81,000 sales denied by the FBI under NICS, nearly 14,000 people appealed, claiming that they were wrongly denied; of cases adjudicated at the time the report was issued, 2,710 denials had been overturned.
- 3,353 felons and others prohibited by law from purchasing firearms were allowed to buy guns over the counter after being mistakenly approved by NICS.

H.B. 245

To its credit H.B. 245 [a Louisiana law that prohibits the transfer of a firearm at a gun show through anyone other than a licensed gun dealer, and which did not pass] recognizes that private individuals cannot obtain access to the

NICS system, thus it proposes allowing the occasional seller or private collector who wishes to sell a gun at a gun show to obtain a background check either through a licensed dealer provided by the gun show promoter or through another willing licensed dealer for a nominal fee. However, this would be like requiring individuals who wish to sell their used cars to conduct the sale through a used car dealer. It would take time away from the dealer's business and put him at risk of losing sales to a third party selling a substitute product at a better price.

Based on these facts, I submit that H.B. 245 would have no measurable impact in reducing violent crime.

A Mean-Spirited Attack on Gun Show Operators

The mean-spirited campaign of vilification against gun show operators, vendors, and customers is unjustifiable. All available data about crime guns show that gun shows play virtually no role in criminal gun acquisition. The so-called "gun show loophole" is a fraud; laws at gun shows are already the same as everywhere else. To impose additional restrictions solely on gun shows is to make laws at gun shows more restrictive than at any other location. Such special legislation would entrap many people at target shooting events, gun club meetings, political meetings, hunting trips, and similar events into unintended criminal violations. The effect is to punish people for exercising their constitutional right to assemble and their right to arms at the same time.

Dave Kopel and Alan Korwin, "Should Gun Shows Be Outlawed?" Second Amendment Project, January 23, 2002. www.davekopel.com.

Perhaps the most important reason to reject expanding the flawed NICS system to private sales at gun shows is that it could actually cause an increase in the victimization of innocents—the very antithesis of the bill's authors' intentions. Studies have shown that criminals fear armed citizens far more than police. Their fear is reasonable since up to 3,000 criminals are lawfully killed each year by armed civilians— more than three times the number killed by the police. An additional 9,000 to 17,000 criminals are wounded by civilians each year. In addition, more than 15 studies have shown that citizens use guns in self-defense between 800,000 and 3.6 million times annually (in the vast majority of cases merely showing the firearm wards off the attack or prevents the crime). Award-winning criminologists Gary Kleck and Mark Gertz estimated that defensive gun uses (DGUs) totaled more than 2.5 million per year. Another study sponsored by the National Institute of Justice and carried out by the Police Foundation found an even greater number of DGUs—approximately 2.73 million a year. Either figure is far larger than the number of crimes committed with firearms each year. Thus, any legislation that discourages or mistakenly disallows legally permitted persons from lawfully purchasing a firearm in a timely manner could place them, and the general public at increased risk from violent crime.

Each law-abiding citizen who is mistakenly delayed or rejected from purchasing a firearm is placed unnecessarily at risk from crime. In the past, this has had deadly results. For instance, in 1995 when Philip Coleman of Shreveport, Louisiana, attempted to purchase a handgun for self-defense the sale was mistakenly rejected. Mr. Coleman appealed the decision, pointing out the error. Mr. Coleman was shot to death outside of his work while his application was still pending. Three days after his murder, the approval of Mr. Coleman's purchase arrived by fax.

Gun control advocates are seeking to close a nonexistent loophole. Logically, this will lead to calls for closing other nonexistent loopholes until all private firearms transfers— even those between family and friends—are under government regulation.

Tightening gun show requirements might make sense if NICS worked as it should and if background checks on private gun sales reduced violent crime, but there is no evidence that either is the case. Rather than expanding the flawed NICS to cover the small number of private sales at gun shows, money could be better spent fixing the NICS and prosecuting the felons who have already purchased guns illegally.

"One could make the case that confronting attackers is, for those who can, something of a civic obligation."

Using Guns Preemptively in Self-Defense Helps Defeat Criminals

A. Barton Hinkle

In 2005 Florida passed a law that expanded on the "castle doctrine," which says that individuals have the right to use deadly force, including firing a gun, when attacked inside their home. Under Florida's new law, individuals can now use deadly force anywhere if attacked. A. Barton Hinkle argues in favor of the law in the following viewpoint. He asserts that if citizens do not stand up to criminals wherever they may confront them, these lawbreakers will have free rein to terrorize honest Americans. Hinkle is the senior editorial writer for the *Richmond Times-Dispatch*.

As you read, consider the following questions:
1. How did the media react to the passage of Florida's stand-your-ground law, according to the author?
2. As cited by Hinkle, of the 266,710 concealed-weapons permits issued, how many were revoked because the individual was charged with a firearms offense?
3. Why does the author consider the stand-your-ground law a Rorschach test?

[F]lorida] governor Jeb Bush signed into law a measure expanding the right to self-defense. Next year [2004] a similar bill could be coming to a legislature near you.

The "Castle Doctrine"

The bill carries the "castle doctrine"—which says a person has the right to use deadly force when attacked inside his home—to any public place where a person happens to be. The bill passed both houses of the state legislature by lopsided margins (unanimously in the Senate, 94-20 in the House), despite lopsided opposition by the state's newspapers. The *Miami Herald* termed it a "macho" law that endorsed the principle of "kill or be killed." The *Sun-Sentinel* said the "trigger-happy" legislature was "getting in touch with its inner Dirty Harry." The *Lakeland Ledger* called the measure "madness" that "codifies machismo."

The National Rifle Association, which championed the measure, plans to lobby for its introduction in every state. "We will start with the red [states, which have voted Republican in recent elections] and move to [the] blue [states, which vote Democratic]," says executive vice president Wayne LaPierre. "In terms of passing it, it is downhill rather than uphill because of all the public support." He has good reason for confidence: The NRA chose Florida to push for the right to carry a concealed weapon, which 38 states now statutorily recognize.

Like the previous Florida fights, the stand-your-ground law, as it is sometimes called, acts like a Rorschach [inkblot] test. It makes conservatives cheer and liberals recoil. The essence of the bill consists of a shift in legal doctrine. Until now, Florida residents who were attacked in public had a duty to use every reasonable means to avoid harm—including running away—before meeting force with force. Under the new doctrine, trying to avoid a confrontation if possible remains probably the wisest course, but retreating is no longer an obligation.

Florida as the Wild West?

To critics, the stand-your-ground measure will turn Florida into the Wild West. Of course, that's what they predicted, erroneously, when Florida passed its concealed-weapons measure. Yet as *The Washington Post* reported a few years later: "In Florida, which adopted a permissive concealed-weapon law in 1987, even critics acknowledge that their worst fears have not been realized. Of 266,710 permits issued in the last eight years, only 19 were revoked because the individual was involved in a crime with a firearm." Indeed, states that adopted right-to-carry laws generally saw a subsequent decrease in robbery and murder. Crime might not have fallen because of the concealed-carry statutes; other factors (demographics, economics) might deserve at least portions of the credit. But neither did the concealed-carry statutes produce the predicted spikes in crime.

Victims and Self-Defense

Between 1993 and 2001, about 61% of all victims of violent crime reported taking a self-defensive measure during the incident.

Most used nonaggressive means, such as trying to escape, getting help, or attempting to scare off or warn the offender. About 13% of victims of violent crime tried to attack or threaten the offender. About 2% of victims of violent crime used a weapon to defend themselves; half of these, about 1% of violent crime victims, brandished a firearm.

All victims' responses to violent crime	100%
Offered no resistance	39.3
Took some action	60.5
Used physical force toward offender	13.0
Attacked/threatened offender without a weapon	10.8
Attacked/threatened offender with a gun	0.7
Attacked/threatened offender with other weapon	1.4
Resisted or captured offender	15.0
Scared or warned off offender	4.2
Persuaded or appeased offender	5.5
Escaped/hid/got away	9.8
Got help or gave alarm	3.9
Reacted to pain or emotion	0.3
Other	8.9
Method of resistance unknown	0.2

Note: Detail may not add to total because of rounding.

Craig Perkins, "Weapon Use and Violent Crime," *National Crime Victimization Survey, 1993–2001*, Bureau of Justice Statistics, U.S. Department of Justice, September 2003, p. 11.

Then again, while pro-gun and anti-gun activists both marshal statistics to suit their views, numbers probably don't change anyone's mind on such matters. Opinions on the use of force are philosophical—if not visceral. Please note that the Florida law makes no reference to guns. It says: "A person does not have a duty to retreat if the person is in a place where he or she has a right to be" and has "the right to stand his or her ground and meet force with force, including deadly force if he or she reasonably believes it is necessary to do so, to prevent death or great bodily harm to himself or herself or another." Deadly force could mean a tire iron or a baseball bat.

It might, in fact, be the case that a given individual's opinions on guns are determined by his thoughts and feelings on aggression and self-defense, rather than vice versa. An analogy to national defense and the War on Terror seems fitting here: After [the September 11, 2001, terrorist attacks], significant chunks of liberal opinion took the view that the appropriate way to reduce the terrorist threat was to ask "Why do they hate us?"—i.e., what must America do to appease Islamofascist extremists so they don't attack again? MoveOn.org opposed not only the war in Iraq but the war in Afghanistan, and *The New Republic*'s Peter Beinart drew incoming fire from the left when he wrote that all serious liberals supported the Afghanistan conflict. The conservative consensus was, by contrast, "You started this fight, but we'll finish it."

There is a strain of liberalism that seems uncomfortable with the idea of fighting back when attacked, as if cowering were a virtue; note the quotes from the Florida newspapers above, or the remarks of Arthur Hayhoe, president of the Florida Coalition to Stop Gun Violence, who called the stand-your-ground bill "mind-boggling in its audacity." Note also that retreating remains an option for those who prefer it; the opponents are upset by the possibility that anyone might not choose to run away.

But most Americans probably agree with NRA lobbyist Marion Hammer, who terms the duty to retreat absurd: "To suggest that you can't defend yourself against a rapist who's trying to drag you into an alley or against a carjacker who's trying to drag you out of your car is nonsense," he said recently. "The ability to protect yourself, your children, or your spouse is important, no matter where you are."

Indeed, one could make the case that confronting attackers is, for those who can, something of a civic obligation. The duty to retreat cedes all power to the aggressors, allowing them to chase the law-abiding from places they have every right to be and offering the lawless the encouragement of triumph. The result is a society in which cretins rule and decent people must run and hide. Florida legislator Arthenia Joyner, who voted against the stand-your-ground bill, warned: "We opened Pandora's Box, and inside that box will be death to some persons." More reasonable minds would reply that when someone comes after you or your family with a knife, Pandora's Box already has been opened—and the law-abiding citizens have every right to shut it.

"It's as if the text of a real bill somehow got transposed with dialogue from a 1970s Dirty Harry paean to vigilantism."

Using Guns Preemptively in Self-Defense Increases Gun Violence

Michelle Cottle

In the following viewpoint Michelle Cottle expresses her opposition to the 2005 Florida stand-your-ground law, which allows an individual to use a gun for self-defense in public places. Cottle asserts that the law will encourage people who would have previously reacted to provocation by moving away to instead threaten to shoot the aggressor. Such vigilantism will only increase gun violence, she contends. Cottle is a senior editor of *New Republic* and has written commentary for CNN, the *New York Times*, *Slate*, *Time*, and the *Atlantic Monthly*.

As you read, consider the following questions:

1. Why is the author conflicted about guns?
2. How has the Bush administration responded to the NRA, in the author's opinion?
3. Despite public support for gun control laws, why does the NRA oppose them, according to Cottle?

D espite my liberal credentials as a Volvo-driving, prochoice, gay-marriage-supporting urban dweller, I admit to an inner conflict when it comes to guns. I grew up surrounded by firearms and the boys who loved them. My father is a bona fide hunting nut who threatened to buy my son a lifetime membership to the National Rifle Association [N.R.A.] for his first birthday. I myself have mowed down a variety of defenseless woodland creatures. I used to be a decent shot with a pistol, and once during the Clinton years, I spearheaded an outing of lefty political scribes for a round of skeet shooting.

But while I appreciate guns, I also appreciate the need for gun laws. Without them, Dad's quip—"A well-armed society is a polite society"—holds true only if your idea of "polite" is something akin to HBO's *Deadwood* or the Sunni triangle [where violence rages in Iraq]. Which is why I'm perturbed by the Florida legislature's decision to pass a bill, signed into law by Governor Jeb Bush last week [May 2005], allowing virtually anyone who feels threatened at any time and in any place to whip out a gun and open fire. The law decrees that a person under attack "has no duty to retreat and has the right to stand his or her ground and meet force with force, including deadly force if he or she reasonably believes it is necessary to do so to prevent death or great bodily harm to himself or herself or another or to prevent the commission of a forcible felony."

"Stand his or her ground"? "Meet force with force"? Wow. It's as if the text of a real bill somehow got transposed with dialogue from a 1970s Dirty Harry paean to vigilantism. I can picture a stressed-out Tampa soccer mom drawing a bead on an approaching panhandler and shrieking, "Go ahead, make my day!"

Gun-control advocates are distraught over this development, predicting a rise in everything from road-rage episodes to gang violence. Gun toters may wrongly assume they have "total immunity from prosecution," said Miami police chief John Timoney. The law's supporters dismiss such concerns as liberal hysteria and extol the bill's passage as a victory for law-abiding citizens. Wayne LaPierre, the N.R.A.'s excruciatingly macho executive vice president, crowed, "[This will] make criminals pause before they commit their next rape, robbery or murder."

A Bad Joke

One of the opponents of the [stand-your-ground] law is the father of a teenage boy who was killed a year and a half ago while playing door-knocking pranks in a Boca Raton, Fla., neighborhood.

Investigators said resident Jay Levin heard something outside his door and when he opened it he saw Mark Drewes. He thought the boy was turning toward him, and he shot him in the back.

Levin pleaded guilty to manslaughter and was sentenced to 52 weekends in jail and probation.

The boy's father, Greg Drewes, opposed the bill because he believes his son's killer would have gone free if it had been in effect at the time of the Boca Raton shooting, the *Palm Beach Post* reported.

"It's a joke. Unbelievable. It's a bad joke," said Drewes of the new law.

"If you shoot somebody in anger, what are you going to say? I made a mistake. I wasn't in any danger. Take me away?" Drewes said. "They're all going to lie. They're all going to say 'I did it to protect myself. I was in fear for my life."

Les Kjos, "Analysis: Florida Gun Law Signed, *The Washington Times*, April 27, 2005.

I don't buy it, Wayne. The Florida courts, like those elsewhere, have long acknowledged that shooting someone in self-defense is, on occasion, a tragic necessity. It's just that, until now, most states have held to the notion that lethal force should be avoided whenever a reasonable alternative, like running away, is safely possible. The recognized exception is when a person's home has been invaded, at which point the homeowner may shoot first and ask questions later—a provision commonly referred to as the "Castle Doctrine." But the N.R.A. and Florida lawmakers apparently felt the definition of one's "castle" needed broadening to include pretty much anywhere a person might happen to wander. Some drunk spoiling for a fight at your favorite bar? Don't "retreat" to another barstool. Flash the .44 Magnum in your shoulder holster and ask the punk if he feels lucky.

Unfortunately, this legislative absurdity is a problem for more than just Florida. A triumphant N.R.A. has vowed to get "stand your ground" laws passed in every state. "We will start with red and move to blue" [conservative states to liberal ones]. LaPierre has declared, adding ominously, "Politicians are putting their career in jeopardy if they oppose this type of bill."

Though irritating, LaPierre's cockiness is perhaps justified. The Bush years have been good to the N.R.A. With Republicans running Washington, cowed Democrats are afraid to utter the words gun control even in the privacy of their homes. As a result, despite polls showing that most Americans support sensible gun laws, the N.R.A. has opposed even popular measures like renewing the 1994 ban on assault weapons (which Congress let lapse last year [2004]). At this point, the N.R.A. won't even support banning the sale of guns to terrorist suspects on the no-fly list. Pressed on the matter, LaPierre has piously asserted, "This is a list that somebody has just put a name on. These people haven't been indicted for anything. They haven't been convicted of anything."

Alas, despite its oft professed commitment to keeping weapons away from the bad guys, the N.R.A. clearly has no use for any gun laws—other than some Wild West, kill-or-be-killed law of the streets. But, hey, if that's the way the gun lobby thinks we should start handling disputes in this country, maybe it's time the Democratic Party stopped agonizing about gun control and started brushing up on its aim—if only for purposes of self-defense. I'd be happy to organize a trip to the skeet range anytime, guys. My Volvo seats five.

"'Safe-storage' laws for guns . . . lead directly to the deaths of both children and adults."

Mandating the Safe Storage of Guns Leaves Homeowners Vulnerable to Criminals

Dave Kopel, Paul Gallant, and Joanne Eisen

According to Dave Kopel, Paul Gallant, and Joanne Eisen in the following viewpoint, laws that regulate the storage of guns in private homes hinder the ability of homeowners to defend themselves against criminals. Moreover, the authors maintain that more children die in household accidents such as drowning than they do by gun violence; thus, in the authors' opinion, safe-storage laws are unnecessary. A prolific writer on the subject of guns and gun rights, Kopel is research director at the Independence Institute, a conservative public policy research organization. Gallant and Eisen are senior fellows at the Independence Institute.

As you read, consider the following questions:

1. According to a 1996 Department of Justice survey of American households, how many guns were loaded and not safely stored?
2. Are fatal gun accidents in the home increasing or decreasing every year, according to Kopel, Gallant, and Eisen?
3. How has vocabulary influenced the debate over gun-storage issues, according to the authors?

We're told that "safe-storage" laws for guns are all about saving the lives of our children. In fact, these laws lead directly to the deaths of both children and adults. The only people to end up safer are violent home intruders.

In a chapter in a book published last month [September 2000], *The Crime Drop in America*, Dr. Garen Wintemute—one of the intellectual stars of the anti-gun movement—commented on "access to firearms" in America.

According to a 1996 Department of Justice survey, 35 to 40 percent of American households have firearms in them. (The true figure may be closer to 1 out of 2 households, since some gun owners may be reluctant to disclose private information to pollsters.) . . . Remarkably, one-third of handguns in the United States—perhaps 20 million guns—were stored loaded and not locked away.

No Clear and Present Danger

Loaded guns just lying around the homes of Americans, ready for action. A clear and present danger to the families in those households? Not according to current safety figures.

In 1994, fatal gun accidents reached the lowest annual level since record-keeping began in 1903. They've dropped even lower each year since.

What should have been "remarkable" to Wintemute is that there were just 20 fatal gun accidents among children under the age of 5 in 1998. Contrast this with phony claims you hear about "10 children a day killed by guns." The greatest part of that factoid comes from gang-related homicides perpetrated by inner-city, 17-to-19-year-old male criminals.

Also contrast the 20 fatal gun accidents for children 0-to-4 with the near 600 children in that same age group who drowned. In fact, more children under the age of 5 drown in 5-gallon buckets of water than are harmed in a firearm accident.

You'd never know this by reading the current fund-raising letter from Handgun Control, Inc. (HCI), which shrieks about parents leaving loaded guns on the dining room table within reach of small children. The letter doesn't point to any actual instances of such dining-room tragedy. Rather it complains that most states don't have a law specifically forbidding it.

In truth, all states have reckless endangerment and negligence laws which apply to guns, drain cleaner, knives, vodka, or anything else that might cause injury in the hands of a small child. Even without an HCI-mandated gun-lock law, parents know plenty of ways to keep items away from children without using mechanical locks.

We are told that "reasonable" trigger-lock laws are the cure for firearm accidents and gun thefts. What we are not told is that trigger-locks won't stop 10-year-olds, who can pop them off with screwdrivers, or break them with hammers. Such locks certainly won't stop determined criminals. So just who is the target of these "reasonable" gun laws, and what's their real purpose?

Rather than saving lives, could it be that trigger-lock laws are intended to condition Americans into believing that firearms aren't acceptable for self-defense, or worth the bother?

What the Research Says

The most up-to-date research on the effect of gun-storage laws comes from Dr. John Lott and Dr. John Whitley in a study scheduled for publication in the April 2001 issue of the *Journal of Law and Economics*. In "Safe Storage Gun Laws: Accidental Deaths, Suicides, and Crime", Lott and Whitley analyzed the effects of safe-storage laws from data spanning nearly 20 years. Their preliminary findings were released on March 29, 2000.

Lott and Whitley found that not only did such laws *not* save lives, they *cost* lives by making it more difficult to have a firearm ready for a sudden emergency. During the first 5 years after the passage of "safe-storage" laws, the group of 15 states that adopted them saw average annual increases of murders (over 300), rapes (3,860), robberies (24,650), and aggravated assaults (over 25,000).

The significant danger of gun-storage laws was brought home in an August [2000] incident in Merced, California, where a pitchfork-wielding man attacked Jessica Carpenter's 7-year-old brother and 9-year-old sister. It's neither a surprise nor a coincidence that the cause of this tragedy went unreported by the national press.

Jessica's father had kept a gun in the home, and his children had learned how to fire it. Jessica, age 14, is a very good shot. But by California law, the gun had to be locked up when the parents weren't home. So, when the murderer attacked, Jessica wasn't able to retrieve the gun to save her siblings. She ran to a neighbor, and begged for help. By the time the police showed up, the 7-year-old boy and the 9-year-old girl had been stabbed to death with the pitchfork.

In the aftermath, the children's great-uncle, Rev. John Hilton, declared that their father was "more afraid of the law than of somebody coming in for his family. He's scared to death of leaving the gun where kids could get it because he's afraid of the law. He's scared to teach his children to defend themselves."

According to California's Dangerous Weapons Control Law, "criminal storage of a firearm in the first degree" is punishable by confinement to state prison for a maximum of 3 years, and/or a fine of up to $10,000.

But it was compliance with California's "safe-storage" laws —and the fear of being prosecuted for their violation—that cost the Carpenter family two of their children.

Lobbying with Lives

When it comes to "safe-storage," the real tragedy is that, despite all the professed concerns about "the children," the anti-self-defense lobby has no qualms in playing politics with the lives of children. Wintemute, who has a much stronger record for intellectual honesty than many other researchers on his side of the gun issue, admits that for "child-access prevention laws . . . at this time there is no good evidence that the laws are effective."

Indeed, there is direct evidence that these are lethal laws. The tragedy in Merced is just one graphic instance of the thousands of additional murders and violent crimes that have resulted from criminals being emboldened by gun-storage laws that turn a family's home into a safe zone for violent predators.

The hidden agenda behind safe-storage laws has nothing to do with safety. First, the anti-gun lobby believes that armed self-defense, by people who are not government employees, is inherently immoral; so preventing families from protecting themselves is a step forward for civilization. The late David Clarke was the leading anti-gun advocate on the Washington, D.C. City Council. He claimed that his efforts to outlaw gun ownership for self-defense "are designed to move this government toward civilization. . . . I don't intend to run the government around the moment of survival."

A Blanket Solution to an Isolated Problem

Exactly where are accidental firearms deaths among children the greatest problem? And, if accidental firearms deaths are not uniformly distributed through all geographic and demographic areas of society, is it appropriate to pass blanket legislation that seeks to solve a problem that doesn't exist through most of our state?

The fact is that the greatest number of accidental firearms deaths and injuries among children occur in urban and inner-city areas. Would it make sense to impose legislation directed at a ghetto problem, on the residents of our suburban and rural counties? Certainly not!

Andy Barniskis, *Gun Owners of America*, February 1998.

Mrs. Sarah Brady, Chair of Handgun Control, Inc., agrees: "To me, the only reason for guns in civilian hands is for sporting purposes." As a direct result of her group's successful lobbying, the California government was emphatically not around at "the moment of survival" for the Carpenter children.

In Canada, gun prohibitionists, such as then–Justice Minister Alan Rock, have used storage laws as a justification for imposing universal gun registration, since registration "will create a sense of accountability on the part of the firearms owner to comply with some of the safe-storage laws that are in effect."

As the next step, the anti-gun lobbies in Canada (who work closely with their American cousins) have begun pushing for "community storage." Rather than keeping your guns in a safe in your home, you would have to keep your guns at a police station. When you wanted to use your gun for the day, you could check it out from the police station.

This latest Canadian ploy isn't really new. Long ago, Sir Walter Raleigh wrote that the "sophisticated and subtle tyrant" will "unarm his people, and store up their weapons, under pretence of keeping them safe."

In the 1950s, one of the most popular sitcoms was *Father Knows Best*. Starring Robert Young as head of the Anderson family, it centered on family values and personal responsibility. The show was not entitled *Government Knows Best*. Half a century later, it's still true that parents, not legislators, know best how to keep their children safe.

Because the vocabulary of the debate has a great influence on the debate's result, people who really care about family safety need to stop using the words "safe storage" when discussing lethal laws like government-storage mandates. These laws turn a family's home into a safe zone for criminals.

"For families who feel safer with a gun for protection, safe storage of firearms and ammunition can reduce the risk of unintentional and self-inflicted firearm injury."

Storing Guns Safely Reduces Accidental Gun Violence

Thomas B. Cole and Reneé M. Johnson

According to Thomas B. Cole and Reneé M. Johnson in the following viewpoint, studies show that storing guns safely can reduce youth suicide rates and unintentional fatalities among children. The authors recommend that firearms be stored locked and unloaded. Statistics indicate that this practice protects both children and adolescents, Cole and Johnson contend. Cole and Johnson are both physicians.

As you read, consider the following questions:

1. In 2002 how many children and adolescents died of firearm suicides and unintentional firearm injuries, as cited by the authors?
2. What does a study in the *Journal of the American Medical Association* show regarding the relationship between youth suicides and safe-storage laws?
3. When is compliance with firearm-storage laws more likely, according to the authors?

The seventh leading "actual," or preventable, cause of death in the United States in 2000 was firearm injury, ranked after tobacco, poor diet and physical activity, alcohol consumption, microbial agents, toxic agents, and motor vehicle injury, and ahead of sexual behavior and illicit drug use. Firearms are present in about one third of US households. Children and adolescents may be tempted to play or practice with firearms, and those who have access to firearms sometimes handle them without adult supervision. Not surprisingly, the presence of a firearm in the home is associated with an increased risk for suicide; the relative risk of unintentional firearm injury is not known.

Firearm Deaths

In 2002, 1057 US children and adolescents ranging in age from less than 1 year to 20 years died of firearm suicide and another 190 of unintentional gunshot wounds. In a King County, Washington, study, household firearms were used in almost one fourth of unintentional shootings of children and adolescents and one third of self-inflicted shootings between 1990 and 1995. More than three fourths of the firearms in this study had been stored in the homes of the injured children, a relative, or a friend. To prevent unsupervised access of children to firearms, 18 states had enacted child access prevention laws as of 2001. These laws make it a crime to store firearms in a manner that allows them to be easily accessed by children and adolescents.

However, locking away firearms from children and adolescents may also limit access to the firearms by their adult owners. Many households keep firearms for protection against potentially violent intruders, and surveys indicate that firearms are often used for this purpose in the United States. Consequently, families may perceive that keeping a gun for protection and protecting their children from firearm injury are equally important.

To appeal to the safety consciousness of gun-owning families with children, groups such as the National Shooting Sports Foundation, the trade association for the firearms and recreational shooting sports industry, and the American Academy of Pediatrics recommend that firearms in the home be stored locked and unloaded to prevent access to them by children. The National Shooting Sports Foundation Web site advises, "Keeping a gun to defend your family makes no sense if that same gun puts your family members or visitors to your home at risk. Many home firearms accidents occur when unauthorized individuals, often visitors, discover loaded firearms that were carelessly left out in the open. . . . Special lockable cases that can be quickly opened only by authorized individuals are options to consider."

Intuitively, storing firearms locked and unloaded should prevent firearm injuries to children who do not intend to harm themselves. Safe storage might also discourage or delay access to firearms by adolescents who do intend to harm themselves, or divert them to less lethal means of self-harm. However, previous studies of household firearms and adolescent suicide have not shown statistically significant associations of specific safe storage practices and a reduced risk of firearm injury in homes with children and adolescents, either because these studies lacked statistical power to examine these associations or did not analyze data for children and adolescents separately from adult data.

How to Store Guns Safely

- Lock your gun. Guns should be stored unloaded, uncocked and securely locked out of sight or reach to minimize the risk that they will be used by unauthorized others such as children, teens, burglars, or the mentally ill or emotionally disturbed. . . .

- Keep the keys to the lock(s) that secure your gun(s) on your key chain and with you at all times. Keep keys out of reach of children and teens. . . .

- Do not store your gun under a bed, mattress or in an unlocked bedroom drawer.

Michigan Partnership to Prevent Gun Violence, "Safe Gun Ownership, Safe Gun Storage," www.mppgv.org.

[However, in a new study reported in the *Journal of the American Medical Association*, D.C.] Grossman et al report that guns stored locked or unloaded were less likely to be used by children or adolescents to shoot themselves or to shoot others unintentionally. To measure the association of specific household firearm storage practices (locking guns, locking ammunition, and keeping guns unloaded), Grossman et al conducted a case-control study of unintentional and self-inflicted firearm injuries to children and adolescents. Each of these safe storage practices was associated with reductions in the relative risk of firearm injury. The protective associations remained strong and statistically significant after controlling for county of residence, ages of children in the home, characteristics of the survey respondents, type of firearm, number of guns stored in the home, and whether the study gun was kept for recreation or protection. Results were similar for suicide attempts and unintentional injuries. Firearm assaults and homicides were not studied because of the difficulty in acquiring accurate data on the source and storage of firearms.

Studying the Effects on Children and Adolescents

More research is needed to determine whether safe storage practices are equally effective for adolescents as for younger children. In theory, suicidal adolescents may be persistent and determined enough to access firearms and ammunition even if safely stored or may kill themselves by other methods. In apparent support of this theory, a national study of adults and adolescents aged 15 years and older found that those who killed themselves with firearms were less likely to have locked or unloaded firearms in their homes than persons who died of other causes, but the protective effect of safe storage declined as the presumed intention to die increased. Grossman et al were unable to determine whether the 5% of children and adolescents in their study who survived suicide attempts died of subsequent attempts after the study. If suicidal children and adolescents in homes with safely stored firearms use alternate methods to kill themselves, then safe gun storage may be viewed as only temporarily successful in preventing suicide.

Despite this limitation, the study by Grossman et al strongly suggests that unsafe firearm storage is associated with firearm suicide and unintentional firearm death. Each method of safe storage of firearm and ammunition examined by Grossman et al was associated with a reduction in unintentional or self-inflicted shooting. Therefore, if physicians can persuade parents to adopt at least 1 safe storage practice, their children's risk of unintentional or self-inflicted firearm injury is likely to decrease. Options for safe storage may facilitate firearm safety counseling and increase compliance with physicians' recommendations.

Social science research on persuasion suggests that the likelihood of compliance is greater if a smaller, more feasible, recommendation can be made when there is resistance to a more substantial recommendation. In terms of firearm storage, the initial, substantial recommendation might be to keep all firearms unloaded, in a locked compartment, secured with an extrinsic safety device, and to keep ammunition locked in a different compartment. If parents are unwilling to comply with all components of this recommendation, the physician could encourage adoption of 1 or 2 of the specific storage practices. Behavioral theory suggests that this type of strategy could allow gun-owning adults to store their firearms in a manner that they might perceive as effective for defensive use and yet foster a safe environment for children.

Reduced Risk

The study by Grossman et al establishes that safe firearm storage is associated with a reduced risk for firearm injury. The next step is to help families make informed decisions about safe storage of firearms, recognizing that keeping children safe is as important to parents who own guns as those who do not. Experience suggests that persuading gun-owning families to store their firearms safely is not an easy task. Educational interventions to promote safe storage of firearms (including physician counseling) have not been successful in the past. Part of the problem may be that safe storage programs may not have been informed by a comprehensive understanding of the determinants of firearm storage practices.

Generating widespread improvement in firearm storage practices will require a commitment to conducting behavioral science research and applying new information to design effective interventions. First, research outlining the determinants of storage practices is needed. Specifically, studies should address parents' risk perceptions about firearm injury to children in conjunction with their beliefs about the effectiveness of guns for defense and motivations underlying parents' firearm storage practices. Surprisingly, little of this information is available. Next, what is learned from behavioral research should be applied to small-scale interventions, using behavioral science theory to guide intervention development. The effectiveness of different strategies for eliciting behavioral change should be evaluated using experimental design. In addition, strategies that have been demonstrated in intervention studies as being effective should be distributed and incorporated into a standard of care. Most families with children and adolescents have chosen not to keep firearms in their homes, but for families who feel safer with a gun for protection, safe storage of firearms and ammunition can reduce the risk of unintentional and self-inflicted firearm injury.

Periodical Bibliography

The following articles have been selected to supplement the diverse views presented in this chapter.

Ronald Brownstein — "A Smarter Way to Control Outbreaks of School Violence," *Washington Post*, March 25, 2005.

H. Sterling Burnett — "Gun Show 'Loophole': More Gun Control Disguised as Crime Control," *American Hunter*, May 2001.

David Codrea — "Safe Schools," *Guns Magazine*, February 2005.

Abigail A. Kohn et al. — "Straight Shooting on Gun Control," *Reason*, May 2005.

John R. Lott Jr. — "If Gun Background Checks Don't Work, Will 'Watch Lists' Be Any More Effective?" *Investor's Business Daily*, March 22, 2005.

John R. Lott Jr. — "Shooting Blanks," *New York Post*, December 29, 2004.

John R. Lott Jr. and Eli Lehrer — "More Gun Control Isn't the Answer," *National Post*, June 15, 2004.

Thomas Sowell — "Gun Control Myths: Part III," *TownHall.com*, November 28, 2002. www.townhall.com.

Lance K. Stell — "The Production of Criminal Violence in America," *Journal of Law, Medicine & Ethics*, Spring 2004.

John Taffin — "The Gun Show Loophole and It Ain't About Politics," *Guns Magazine*, September 2004.

Helen Thomas — "Hats Off to John McCain's Effort to Close the Gun Show Loophole," *Seattle Post Intelligencer*, December 5, 2001.

Timothy Wheeler — "A Light Goes On at the CDC," *National Review Online*, October 22, 2003. www.nationalreview.com.

For Further Discussion

Chapter 1

1. Both Robert Spitzer and James B. Jacobs offer statistics on the problem of gun violence in the United States. Do you find these numbers alarming enough to justify more stringent gun laws? Or do you accept Jacobs's assurances that the extent of gun violence has been exaggerated? Explain.

2. Robert Spitzer provides statistics that show that the United States has a much higher rate of gun violence than other developed nations. Do you think these higher rates are due to the number of guns owned in America or because of some other factor? Explain.

3. Josh Sugarmann argues that youths have easy access to firearms. Do you believe that guns are widely available to American youth? If so, is this availability a factor in the high rates of youth gun violence? What are other contributing factors?

4. Mike Males maintains that the media exaggerate the prevalence of youth gun violence in America. Do you believe the media provide a one-sided view of violent youths in America? Provide examples that you have observed.

5. Should Americans enact gun control measures to protect America from terrorists, as suggested by Mark Benjamin? Or, as Wayne LaPierre and James Jay Baker assert, is the problem exaggerated for political reasons? Explain.

Chapter 2

1. After reviewing evidence presented by Robert A. Levy and David Hemenway, do you believe owning a gun contributes to gun violence or protects gun owners from criminals?

2. Based on the viewpoints presented by Steve Newton and Eric W. Alexy, do you think concealed weapons laws increase or decrease levels of gun violence? In your opinion, should individuals be allowed to carry concealed weapons? Explain your answer.

3. John R. Lott Jr. argues that Americans should be allowed to own assault weapons. Do you believe that Americans should have the right to own assault weapons? Why or why not?

Chapter 3

1. Based on viewpoints presented by the Brady Center to Prevent Gun Violence and Dorothy Anne Seese, do you feel that gun control laws infringe on the Second Amendment right of Amer-

icans? Why or why not? Use evidence cited in the viewpoints to support your answer.

2. After reading all viewpoints in this chapter, do you believe the Second Amendment endorses a collective or individual right to bear arms? Explain your answer, citing authors in this chapter who support your view.

Chapter 4

1. After reading the viewpoints by David Hemenway and Steve Pudlo, do you believe more gun control laws are needed? If so, what kind of laws would you support? If not, please explain your position.

2. Do you feel it is important to close the gun-show loophole, as the Consumer Federation of America recommends? Or, like H. Sterling Burnett, do you have other solutions to the problem? Explain.

3. A. Barton Hinkle believes individuals have the right to defend themselves with a gun anywhere, not just in the home. Do you agree or disagree? What are the implications of stand-your-ground laws?

Organizations to Contact

American Civil Liberties Union (ACLU)
125 Broad St., 18th Fl., New York, NY 10004
(212) 944-9800 • fax: (212) 869-9065
Web site: www.aclu.org

The ACLU is an organization that works to defend the rights and principles delineated in the Declaration of Independence and the U.S. Constitution. It champions the collective interpretation of the Second Amendment; in other words, it believes that the Second Amendment does not guarantee the individual right to own and bear firearms. Consequently, the organization believes that gun control is constitutional and necessary in some instances. The ACLU publishes the semiannual *Civil Liberties* in addition to policy statements and reports.

Brady Center to Prevent Handgun Violence
1250 Eye St. NW, Suite 802, Washington, DC 20005
(202) 289-7319 • fax: (202) 408-1851
Web site: www.bradycenter.org • www.gunlawsuits.org

The Center to Prevent Handgun Violence was renamed the Brady Center to Prevent Handgun Violence in 2001. The organization also encompasses the Brady Campaign to Prevent Handgun Violence (formerly Handgun Control, Inc.), the Legal Action Center, and the Million Mom March. The Brady Center aims to educate the public about gun violence, enact and enforce reasonable gun regulation, and reform the gun industry through litigation. The Brady Campaign works to enact and enforce sensible gun laws, regulations, and public policies through grassroots activism. It also works to elect public officials who support reasonable gun control legislation and to increase public awareness of gun violence. The Legal Action Center provides free legal representation for victims in lawsuits against gun manufacturers, dealers, and owners, and provides updates on recent gun lawsuits. The Million Mom March is a nonpartisan organization that fights to prevent gun violence.

Cato Institute
1000 Massachusetts Ave. NW, Washington, DC 20001
(202) 842-0200 • fax: (202) 842-3490
Web site: www.cato.org

The Cato Institute is a libertarian public-policy research foundation. It evaluates government policies and offers reform proposals and commentary on its Web site. Its publications include the Cato

Policy Analysis series of reports, which have covered topics such as "Fighting Back: Crime, Self-Defense, and the Right to Carry a Handgun" and "Trust the People: The Case Against Gun Control." It also publishes the magazine *Regulation*, the *Cato Policy Report*, and numerous book-length studies.

Citizens Committee for the Right to Keep and Bear Arms (CCRKBA)
12500 NE Tenth Pl., Bellevue, WA 98005
(206) 454-4911 • fax: (206) 451-3959
e-mail: AdminForWeb@ccrkba.org • Web site: www.ccrkba.org

The CCRKBA is a gun rights organization that believes that the Second Amendment protects the right of individuals to buy guns. It disseminates gun rights information and lobbies legislators to prevent the passage of gun control laws. The CCRKBA also sponsors the Citizen Action Project, which encourages individuals to get involved in the fight to preserve individual gun rights. The committee is affiliated with the Second Amendment Foundation and publishes several magazines, including *Gun Week, Women & Guns*, and *Gun News Digest*.

Coalition to Stop Gun Violence (CSGV)
1023 Fifteenth St. NW, Suite 301, Washington, DC 20005
(202) 408-0061
Web site: www.csgv.org

The CSGV and its sister organization, the Educational Fund to Stop Gun Violence, work to reduce gun violence and curb the power of the gun lobby through grassroots activism, a progressive gun control legislative agenda, and litigation against gun manufacturers. The coalition works with many other gun control organizations to lobby at the local, state, and federal level to ban the sale of handguns to individuals and to institute licensing and registration of all firearms. Its publications include various informational sheets on gun violence and the *Annual Citizens' Conference to Stop Gun Violence Briefing Book*, a compendium of gun control fact sheets, arguments, and resources.

Handgun-Free America
1600 Wilson Blvd., Suite 800, Arlington, VA 22209
(703) 465-0474 • fax: (703) 465-5603
e-mail: info@handgunfree.org • Web site: www.handgunfree.org

Founded in 2002, Handgun-Free America is a membership-based, nonprofit organization dedicated to the effort to ban private handgun ownership in the United States. It disseminates information on critical gun issues, such as the assault weapons ban, school and workplace shootings, and safe-storage laws.

Independence Institute
13952 Denver West Parkway, Suite 400, Denver, CO 80401
(303) 279-6536 • fax: (303) 279-4176
e-mail: Anne@i2i.org • Web site: http://i2i.org
The Independence Institute is a public-policy think tank that supports gun ownership as both a civil liberty and a constitutional right. Through the institute's policy centers, it addresses subjects of importance through policy papers, opinion pieces, and special events.

National Crime Prevention Council (NCPC)
1000 Connecticut Ave. NW, 13th Fl., Washington, DC 20036
(202) 466-6272 • fax: (202) 296-1356
e-mail: webmaster@ncpc.org • Web site: www.ncpc.org
A branch of the U.S. Department of Justice, the NCPC develops and implements programs that teach Americans how to reduce gun crime and to ultimately address the causes of gun violence. It provides readers with information on gun control and publishes educational materials on the subject of gun violence. NCPC's publications include the newsletter *Catalyst* and the book *Reducing Gun Violence: What Communities Can Do.*

National Rifle Association (NRA)
11250 Waples Mill Rd., Fairfax, VA 22030
(703) 267-1000 • fax: (703) 267-3989
Web site: www.nra.org
The NRA is America's largest organization of gun owners and the primary lobbying group for those who oppose gun control laws. The organization believes that gun control laws violate the U.S. Constitution and do nothing to reduce crime. In addition to its monthly magazines *America's 1st Freedom*, *American Rifleman*, *American Hunter*, *InSights*, and *Shooting Sports USA*, the NRA publishes numerous books, bibliographies, reports, and pamphlets on gun ownership, gun safety, and gun control.

Second Amendment Foundation (SAF)
12500 NE Tenth Pl., Bellevue, WA 98005
(425) 454-7012 • fax: (425) 451-3959
e-mail: AdminForWeb@saf.org • Web site: www.saf.org
SAF is dedicated to informing Americans about their Second Amendment right to keep and bear firearms. It believes that gun control laws violate this right. The foundation runs an attorney re-

ferral service for individuals in need of the services of a pro–gun rights attorney. It publishes the weekly newspaper *Gun Week*, the monthly newsletter *The Gottlieb-Tartaro Report*, the gun magazine for women entitled *Women & Guns*, and the yearly *Journal on Firearms and Public Policy*.

U.S. Department of Justice
Office of Justice Programs
810 Seventh St. NW, Washington, DC 20531
(202) 732-3277
Web site: www.ojp.usdoj.gov

The Department of Justice protects citizens by maintaining effective law enforcement, crime prevention, crime detection, and prosecution and rehabilitation of offenders. Through its Office of Justice Programs, the department operates the National Institute of Justice, the Office of Juvenile Justice and Delinquency Prevention, and the Bureau of Justice Statistics. Its publications include fact sheets, research packets, bibliographies, and the semiannual journal *Juvenile Justice*.

Violence Policy Center (VPC)
1730 Rhode Island Ave. NW, Suite 1014, Washington, DC 20036
(202) 822-8200 • fax: (202) 822-8202
e-mail: info@vpc.org • Web site: www.vpc.org

The VPC is an educational foundation that conducts research on gun violence and works to educate the public concerning the dangers of guns and supports gun control measures. The center's recent publications include *United States of Assault Weapons; Really Big Guns, Even Bigger Lies;* and *Firearms Production in America.*

Bibliography of Books

Michael A. Bellesiles — *Arming America: The Origins of a National Gun Culture.* New York: Alfred A. Knopf, 2000.

Shay Bilchik — *Reducing Youth Gun Violence: An Overview of Programs and Initiatives Program Report.* Collingdale, PA: Diane, 2004.

John M. Bruce and Clyde Wilcox — *The Changing Politics of Gun Control.* Lanham: MD: Rowman & Littlefield, 1998.

Philip J. Cook and Jens Ludwig — *Gun Violence: The Real Costs.* New York: Oxford University Press, 2000.

Wendy Cukier and Victor W. Sidel — *The Global Gun Epidemic: From Saturday Night Specials to AK-47s.* Westport, CT: Praeger, 2006.

Alexander Deconde — *Gun Violence in America: The Struggle for Control.* Boston: Northeastern University Press, 2003.

Susan Dudley Gold — *Gun Control.* New York: Benchmark Books, 2004.

David Hemenway — *Private Guns, Public Health.* Ann Arbor: University of Michigan Press, 2004.

David M. Kennedy, Anthony A. Braga, and Anne M. Piehl — *Reducing Gun Violence: The Boston Project's Operation Ceasefire.* Collingdale, PA: Diane, 2004.

Gary Kleck — *Point Blank: Guns and Violence in America.* New York: A. de Gruyter, 2005.

Gary Kleck and Don B. Kates Jr. — *Armed: New Perspectives on Gun Control.* Amherst, NY: Prometheus Books, 2001.

Wayne LaPierre — *Guns, Freedom, and Terrorism.* Nashville, TN: WND Books, 2003.

Wayne LaPierre and James Jay Baker — *Shooting Straight: Telling the Truth About Guns in America.* Washington, DC: Regnery, 2002.

Barbara Long — *Gun Control and the Right to Bear Arms.* Berkeley Heights, NJ: Enslow, 2002.

John R. Lott Jr. — *Bias Against Guns.* Washington, DC: Regnery, 2003.

John R. Lott Jr. — *More Guns, Less Crime: Understanding Crime and Gun-Control Laws.* Chicago: University of Chicago Press, 1998.

Terry O'Neill — *Gun Control.* San Diego: Greenhaven Press, 2000.

Robert J. Spitzer	*The Politics of Gun Control.* 3rd ed. Washington, DC: CQ Press, 2004.
Peter Squires	*Gun Culture or Gun Control: Firearms, Violence, and Society.* New York: Routledge, 2000.
Josh Sugarmann	*Every Handgun Is Aimed at You: The Case for Banning Handguns.* New York: New Press, 2001.
George Tita et al.	*Reducing Gun Violence: Results from an Intervention in East Los Angeles.* Santa Monica, CA: Rand, 2003.
Aaron Zelman and Richard W. Stevens	*Death by "Gun Control": The Human Cost of Victim Disarmament.* Hartford, WI: Mazel Freedom Press, 2001.

Index

Second Amendment Committee, 121
Seese, Dorothy Anne, 137
self-defense, use of firearms for, 35–36,
    88, 97, 100, 171, 174
September 11, 2001, attacks, 13
Simmons, Robert, 127
smart guns, 145
Smith, Tom W., 96, 104
Sowell, Thomas, 101
Spencer, Brenda, 53
Spitzer, Robert, 12, 18, 125
stand-your-ground law, 173, 178
Stearns, Cliff, 73
Steber, Michael J., 19
Stolberg, Sheryl, 51
Stupak, Bart, 56
Sugarmann, Josh, 37
suicide(s), 25, 89
    prevalence of, 41, 57–58
    safe-storage laws and, 190–91
    studies on measures to reduce, are
        lacking, 59–60
    rate in U.S. vs. other countries,
        29–30, 64–65
    rural, demographics of, 63–64
Sullivan, Randall, 48, 51
Sun-Sentinel (newspaper), 173
survey(s)
    on closing gun show loophole, 162
    on laws regulating gun sales, 152
    on right to be armed, 135
    on safety at school, 46

Task Force on Gun Violence of the
    American Bar Association, 148
"Teen Suicides and Guns" (Handgun-
    Free America), 57
terrorists
    gun shows are not a source of
        weapons for, 77–79

suspected, are not disqualified from
    buying guns, 74–75
Thomas, Clarence, 140
Tiahrt, Todd, 74
Time (magazine), 54
Timoney, John, 178
trigger locks, mandatory, 29, 145, 183

United States v. Emerson (1998), 116,
    119–20
United States v. Hale (1992), 134
United States v. Miller (1939), 116, 132,
    134
United States v. Nelson (1988), 135
USA PATRIOT Act (2001), 69

Vince, Joe, 71–72
Violence Policy Center, 84, 113
Volokh, Eugene, 119

Wade, Drew, 75
Walton, Rodd, 68
war on terror, gun lobby vs., 69
Washington Post (newspaper), 174
Whitley, John, 183
Willdorf, Barry S., 123
Wintemute, Garen, 182, 184
World Health Organization (WHO),
    65

Yale Law Review, 119
Yellow Ribbon Foundation, 59
"Youth Firearm-Related Violence Fact
    Sheet" (National Youth Violence
    Prevention Resource Center), 41
Youth Handgun Safety Act (1994), 41
youths. *See* children/adolescents
Youth Today (magazine), 48

Zimring, Frank, 32